THE OFFICE ALCHEMIST

MASTER THE ART AND SCIENCE OF CAREER TRANSFORMATION

ANUPAM PETER

ISBN
Paperback 979-8-89673-494-9
Hardcase 979-8-89699-457-2

Warning

This book may challenge your current perspectives on career growth and development. The strategies and insights presented herein require dedication, hard work, and a willingness to adapt. Proceed with an open mind and a commitment to transforming your professional life.

Heads Up! This book is not a magic formula for overnight success. Career growth is a journey, and the principles outlined here will require effort, patience, and persistence. Be prepared to confront your fears, biases, and limitations.

Be Prepared for a Career Awakening! The insights and strategies in this book may disrupt your comfort zone, spark new passions, and ignite a sense of purpose. Embrace the transformation, and get ready to unlock your full potential.

Important Notice: The advice and guidance offered in this book are general in nature and not tailored to individual circumstances. Readers should consult with career professionals or mentors for personalized advice.

Dedication

To every individual seeking purpose and fulfilment in their professional journey,

This book is dedicated to you, with the hope that its pages will illuminate your path, spark clarity, and empower you to unlock your full potential.

May the insights and guidance within these pages inspire you to dream boldly, work wisely, and live a life of meaningful contribution.

To my family, whose unwavering support and love fuelled my passion for helping others navigate their careers.

To the countless individuals who have shared their stories, struggles, and successes with me, thank you for trusting me with your journeys.

May this book be a catalyst for positive change, helping you discover your strengths, overcome obstacles, and thrive in your chosen path.

To those who dare to dream, this book is dedicated to helping you turn your passions into purposeful careers. May your journey be filled with growth, learning, and fulfillment. I remember my own struggles to find direction and purpose. This book is a culmination of my experiences, successes, and setbacks. It's a testament to the power of perseverance and self-discovery. May you find inspiration, guidance, and motivation within these pages. May you unlock your full potential and create a career that brings joy, satisfaction, and lasting impact.

To my mentors, colleagues, and friends who shared their expertise and experiences, I extend my deepest gratitude. This book wouldn't have been possible without your contributions. To anyone facing career uncertainty or adversity, may this book offer hope, resilience, and practical strategies to overcome obstacles and thrive. May you find comfort in knowing you're not alone in your struggles. May you discover your strengths, passions, and purpose, and may your career be a source of joy, fulfilment, and lasting impact.

To career professionals seeking growth, transition, or advancement, this book is dedicated to providing valuable insights, strategic guidance, and actionable advice. May you develop a clear vision for your career, identify opportunities, and create a roadmap for success. May you stay ahead of the curve, adapt to industry trends, and continuously develop your skills. May your career be a testament to your expertise, leadership, and commitment to excellence.

Contents

Preface

As I sit down to write this preface, I am reminded of the countless individuals I've met who are struggling to find purpose, direction, and fulfilment in their careers. From fresh graduates eager to make their mark, to seasoned professionals seeking a mid-career pivot, and those looking to revive their careers after a break, the quest for meaningful work is a universal aspiration.

My own journey has been a testament to the power of perseverance, self-discovery, and strategic decision-making. From navigating the ups and downs of my own career path to guiding others through theirs, I've learned that success is not solely defined by titles, salaries, or prestige. Rather, it's the alignment of one's passions, values, and strengths with their professional pursuits.

This book is the culmination of my experiences, insights, and expertise, distilled into practical, actionable advice for individuals at every stage of their career journey. Whether you're just starting out, seeking to revitalize your current role, or embarking on a new chapter, this book is designed to empower you with the tools, strategies, and confidence to achieve your goals.

Through these pages, I share my own story, as well as those of numerous individuals who have bravely navigated career transitions, overcome obstacles, and achieved remarkable success. Their testimonies serve as a reminder that career growth is a continuous process, marked by twists, turns, and opportunities for growth.

The book is organized into sections that cater to diverse needs and aspirations. For interns and freshers, I offer guidance on crafting a strong foundation, building professional networks, and developing essential skills. For mid-level professionals, I provide strategies for career advancement, leadership development, and navigating organizational politics. For those seeking to revive their careers, I share insights on updating skills, leveraging experience, and exploring new opportunities.

Throughout the book, you'll find self-styled tips, gleaned from my own experiences and those of others, to help you:

1. Identify and leverage your strengths

2. Develop a growth mindset

3. Build resilience and adaptability

4. Foster meaningful professional relationships

5. Navigate career transitions with confidence

6. Cultivate a personal brand that showcases your unique value proposition

My goal is not to provide a one-size-fits-all solution but to offer a comprehensive guide that acknowledges the complexities and nuances of modern careers. I aim to inspire, motivate, and equip you with the knowledge and skills necessary to thrive in an ever-evolving work landscape.

As you embark on this journey, I invite you to approach these pages with an open mind, a willingness to learn, and a commitment to your own growth. Remember, your career is a unique narrative, waiting to be written. This book is merely a catalyst, designed to spark reflection, ignite passion, and empower you to author your own success story.

Thank you for joining me on this journey. I look forward to being your guide, mentor, and companion as you navigate the twists and turns of your career path.

Acknowledgement

As I reflect on the journey of writing this book, I am filled with gratitude for the incredible people who have supported me every step of the way. This project would not have been possible without the love, encouragement, and expertise of numerous individuals, and I am honoured to acknowledge their contributions.

First and foremost, I want to express my deepest gratitude to my beloved wife, Meetu. Your unwavering support, patience, and love have been my driving force throughout this journey. You have been my rock, my confidante, and my biggest cheerleader, always believing in me and pushing me to give my best. I am forever grateful for your sacrifices, your listening ear, and your unrelenting encouragement. This book is as much yours as it is mine, and I dedicate it to you with all my love.

To the team at Notion Press, my publisher, I extend my sincerest appreciation for their professionalism, expertise, and dedication to bringing this project to life. From the initial discussions to the final proofreading, your team has been a pleasure to work with. Your enthusiasm and commitment to quality have been instrumental in shaping this book into a reality. Thank you for believing in my work and for your tireless efforts to make it shine.

To my parents, I thank you for instilling in me the values of hard work, perseverance, and resilience. Your guidance, love, and blessings have shaped me into the person I am today. Your sacrifices and unwavering support have allowed me to pursue my dreams, and I am forever grateful. This book is a testament to your influence in my life, and I hope it makes you proud.

I would also like to thank my friends, family, and colleagues who have supported me throughout this journey. Your encouragement, feedback, and insights have been invaluable. Your presence in my life has made this journey richer and more meaningful.

In addition, I want to acknowledge the numerous individuals who have shared their stories, experiences, and expertise with me. Your contributions have enriched this book and made it more relatable and practical. I am grateful for your trust and willingness to share your journeys with me.

Lastly, I want to express my gratitude to myself. Writing this book has been a transformative journey, one that has pushed me to grow, learn, and reflect on my own experiences. It has been a labour of love, and I am proud of the person I have become through this process.

As I close this acknowledgement, I am filled with a sense of gratitude and humility. I know that this book is not just mine, but a collective effort of many individuals who have contributed to its creation. I hope that it will inspire, motivate, and empower readers to navigate their own career journeys with confidence and purpose. Thank you to everyone who has made this book possible.

Part 1

Assessing Your Career

1

Awakening to Change: Recognizing the Need for Transformation

"Change is the only constant in life."

– Heraclitus

Have you ever felt stuck in your career, like you're running on a treadmill but getting nowhere? You're not alone. Many professionals experience feelings of stagnation, dissatisfaction, or restlessness at some point in their careers.

In this chapter, we'll explore the signs that indicate it's time for a career transformation. We'll delve into why people resist change and the consequences of staying in a stagnant career. Finally, we'll discuss the benefits of embracing transformation and provide practical strategies for initiating change.

Recognizing the Signs of Stagnation

How do you know when it's time for a career transformation? Look for these telltale signs:

1. Lack of challenge: You feel underutilized, bored, or unchallenged in your role.

2. Limited growth opportunities: You've plateaued, with no clear path for advancement.

3. Mismatched values: Your personal values no longer align with your company's or industry's.

4. Burnout: Chronic stress, exhaustion, or cynicism have become your norm.

5. Dissatisfaction: You feel unhappy, unfulfilled, or disconnected from your work.

Why We Resist Change

Despite these signs, many people hesitate to make a change. Why?

1. Fear of uncertainty: The unknown can be daunting.

2. Comfort zone: You may feel comfortable, despite being unhappy.

3. Investment: You've invested time, energy, and resources in your current career.

4. Identity: Your career closely ties to your sense of self.

The Consequences of Staying Stagnant

Staying in a stagnant career can have severe consequences:

1. Declining motivation: Your passion and energy wane.

2. Decreased productivity: Performance suffers due to lack of engagement.

3. Poor physical and mental health: Chronic stress affects well-being.

4. Missed opportunities: You may overlook better-suited career paths.

The Benefits of Transformation

Embracing transformation can bring numerous benefits:

1. Renewed purpose: Aligning your career with your values and passions.

2. Increased fulfilment: Doing work that brings joy and satisfaction.

3. Growth and learning: Expanding skills and knowledge.

4. Improved well-being: Enhanced physical and mental health.

Initiating Change

Ready to start your transformation journey? Take these first steps:

1. Self-reflection: Identify your values, strengths, and passions.

2. Exploration: Research new career paths and industries.

3. Networking: Connect with professionals in desired fields.

4. Skill development: Invest in courses or training.

Steps to Recognize and Act on the Need for Change

1. **Evaluate Current Circumstances:** Identify what's working and what isn't.

2. **Set Clear Goals:** Define what success looks like post-transformation.

3. **Take Small Steps:** Change doesn't have to be drastic; incremental improvements can lead to significant results over time.

4. **Seek Support:** Engage with mentors, coaches, or industry experts who can guide you through the process.

Real-Life Examples of Transformation

Consider individuals who've successfully pivoted in their careers or businesses that reinvented themselves to adapt to market changes:

- A graphic designer learning UX/UI design to stay relevant in a digital-first world.

- A traditional bookstore transforming into a community hub offering experiences rather than just products.

These examples highlight the power of recognizing the need for change early and acting decisively.

Conclusion

Recognizing the need for transformation is the first step toward elevating your career and life. Acknowledge the signs of stagnation, overcome resistance, and embrace the benefits of change.

In the next chapter, we'll delve into discovering your North Star - uncovering your true career purpose.

Reflection Exercise

Take a few minutes to reflect on your current career:

1. What signs of stagnation resonate with you?

2. What fears or concerns hold you back from making a change?

3. What values, strengths, or passions do you want to prioritize in your next career chapter?

Action Plan

1. Schedule time for self-reflection and exploration.

2. Research resources for skill development and networking.

3. Identify potential mentors or career coaches.

2

Discovering Your North Star - Uncovering Your True Career Purpose

. . . .

"Your purpose is the reason you are here on earth. Your passion is the fire that drives you."

– Fabienne Fredrickson

. . . .

In Chapter 1, we explored the signs of stagnation and the importance of recognizing the need for transformation. Now, we'll delve deeper into discovering your North Star - uncovering your true career purpose.

Understanding Career Purpose

Your career purpose is the intersection of your:

1. Values: What matters most to you?

2. Passions: What activities make you come alive?

3. Strengths: What are your natural talents and skills?

4. Impact: How do you want to make a difference?

Uncovering Your Values

Values are the foundation of your career purpose. Reflect on:

1. What motivates you?

2. What do you stand for?

3. What do you believe in?

What Is a Career North Star?

Your North Star is your guiding light—a clear sense of purpose that defines what you want to achieve and why. Unlike short-term goals or fleeting ambitions, your North Star represents your deeper aspirations, values, and passions. It provides direction in the face of uncertainty and serves as a benchmark for your decisions.

For instance, someone with a North Star of "empowering underserved communities through education" may pursue careers in teaching, social work, or nonprofit leadership.

Why Finding Your North Star Matters

Many people drift through their careers, moving from one opportunity to the next without a clear sense of purpose. This often leads to dissatisfaction, burnout, and a feeling of being "stuck." Conversely, those who discover and align with their North Star experience:

1. **Greater Motivation:** Knowing your purpose gives you the drive to persevere through challenges.

2. **Clarity in Decision-Making:** It becomes easier to say yes to opportunities aligned with your purpose and no to distractions.

3. **Fulfilment:** A purpose-driven career leads to a deeper sense of satisfaction and achievement.

Steps to Uncover Your True Career Purpose

1. **Reflect on Your Passions**

2. Think about the activities, subjects, or causes that ignite your enthusiasm. Ask yourself:

- What tasks do I lose track of time doing?

- What issues do I care deeply about?

For example, if you love solving complex problems, a career in data analysis or engineering might align with your purpose.

1. **Identify Your Core Values**

   Values are the principles that guide your decisions and actions. Common values include creativity, freedom, helping others, and innovation. Understanding your values can help you choose a career that feels authentic and meaningful.

2. **Examine Your Strengths**

   Consider your natural talents and the skills you've developed over time. Are you great at connecting with people, analyzing data, or creating art? Your strengths often point toward careers where you can excel.

3. **Explore Your Impact**

   Purpose often lies at the intersection of what you love, what you're good at, and how you can make a positive impact. Reflect on how your work can contribute to others' lives or solve real-world problems.

4. **Listen to Your Intuition**

   While logic and analysis are important, your instincts can also guide you toward what feels right. Pay attention to what excites and energizes you.

Tools to Help Discover Your North Star

- **Journaling:** Regularly write about your career goals, dreams, and challenges to gain clarity.

- **Personality Assessments**

- **Mentorship:** Seek guidance from mentors who have experience in areas you're exploring.

Overcoming Common Challenges in Discovering Purpose

1. **Fear of Change:** Leaving a stable but unfulfilling career can be daunting. Remember that growth often requires stepping out of your comfort zone.

2. **External Pressure:** Ignore societal or familial expectations that don't align with your values. Your career is your journey.

3. **Impatience:** Discovering your North Star takes time. Be patient and trust the process.

Common values include

1. Creativity

2. Autonomy

3. Helping others

4. Innovation

5. Stability

6. Respect

7. Fairness

8. Freedom

Exploring Your Passions

Passions fuel your enthusiasm and energy. Ask yourself

1. What activities make me lose track of time?

2. What topics do I enjoy learning about?

3. What hobbies bring me joy?

Consider your

1. Childhood passions

2. Hobbies

3. Volunteer work

4. Favourite books or podcasts

Identifying Your Strengths

Strengths are your natural talents and skills. Consider

1. What are your innate abilities?

2. What skills have you developed over time?

3. What do others appreciate about you?

Use tools like

1. StrengthsFinder

2. Skill assessments

Defining Your Impact

The impact is the difference you want to make. Reflect on

1. What problems do you want to solve?

2. What industry or field aligns with your values?

3. What kind of legacy do you want to leave?

Career Purpose Exercises

Take time to complete these exercises

1. Values Assessment: Rank your top values.

2. Passion Profiler: List activities that ignite your passion.

3. Strengths Finder: Identify your natural talents.

4. Impact Statement: Craft a statement outlining your desired impact.

Crafting Your Career Purpose Statement

Combine your insights from the exercises above to create a concise statement:

Example: "I empower entrepreneurs through innovative marketing solutions, fostering creativity and growth."

Benefits of a Clear Career Purpose

1. Direction: Clarity on your career path.

2. Motivation: Increased enthusiasm and energy.

3. Focus: Prioritization of meaningful activities.

4. Fulfilment: Alignment with your values and passions.

Overcoming Common Obstacles

1. Fear of uncertainty

2. Lack of clarity

3. Self-doubt

4. External expectations

5. Limited resources

Living Your Purpose

Once you've uncovered your North Star, the next step is to align your actions with it. This might involve pursuing new opportunities, acquiring skills, or even making a career pivot. To stay on track, consistently evaluate your decisions against your purpose.

Conclusion

Discovering your North Star - your true career purpose - illuminates your path forward. By understanding your values, passions, strengths, and impact, you'll make intentional decisions, aligning your career with your deepest aspirations.

In the next chapter, we'll explore evaluating your current career and identifying areas for improvement.

Reflection Exercise

1. What values, passions, strengths, and impact align with your career purpose?
2. How does your current career align with your purpose?
3. What adjustments can you make to align with your purpose?

Action Plan

1. Schedule time for self-reflection.
2. Research resources for values, passions, and strengths assessments.
3. Craft your career purpose statement.

Call to Action

Your North Star is waiting to be discovered. Take the time to reflect, explore, and connect with what truly matters to you. Once you uncover your purpose, you'll find the clarity and motivation to build a career that not only succeeds but also fulfils you.

Ready to start your journey? Begin today by asking yourself: What do I truly want, and how can I make it happen?

By embracing your North Star, you'll navigate your career transformation with clarity, purpose, and passion.

Additional Resources

1. "The 7 Habits of Highly Effective People" by Stephen Covey

2. "StrengthsFinder" by Tom Rath

3. "The Purpose Driven Life" by Rick Warren

3

Career Checkup - Evaluating Your Current Path

"The biggest adventure you can take is to live the life of your dreams."

– Oprah Winfrey

In Chapter 2, we discovered your North Star - your true career purpose. Now, we'll conduct a comprehensive Career Checkup, evaluating your current path to identify areas for improvement.

Just as you go for regular health checkups to ensure your well-being, a career checkup is essential for assessing whether your professional life is on track. It's a structured process to evaluate your current job, goals, and growth opportunities, allowing you to make informed decisions about your future. This chapter explores why career evaluations matter, how to conduct one, and what to do if you discover you need a change.

Why Evaluate Your Current Career?

Evaluating your current career helps you

1. Identify strengths and weaknesses
2. Recognize areas for growth and development
3. Align your current role with your career purpose
4. Make informed decisions about staying or transitioning
5. Enhance job satisfaction and engagement
6. Improve work-life balance
7. Increase career advancement opportunities

The Career Checkup Framework

Assess your current career across these dimensions

1. Job Satisfaction: How fulfilled are you in your role?
2. Skills Utilization: Are you using your strengths and skills?
3. Work-Life Balance: Is your personal life suffering?
4. Career Advancement: Are growth opportunities available?
5. Company Culture: Does the organization align with your values?
6. Compensation and Benefits: Are your financial needs met?
7. Professional Development: Are you learning and growing?

Job Satisfaction Assessment

Evaluate your

1. Role clarity

2. Autonomy

3. Feedback and recognition

4. Challenge and engagement

5. Compensation and benefits

6. Work environment

7. Colleague relationships

Skills Utilization Evaluation

Assess

1. Skill alignment with strengths

2. Opportunities for skill development

3. Skill obsolescence

4. Transferable skills

5. Skill gaps

Work-Life Balance Analysis

Consider

1. Time management

2. Boundary setting

3. Self-care practices

4. Support system

5. Flexibility

Career Advancement Evaluation

Assess

1. Clear career path
2. Mentorship opportunities
3. Training and development
4. Networking opportunities
5. Performance feedback

Company Culture Assessment

Evaluate

1. Values Alignment
2. Leadership style
3. Communication openness
4. Diversity and inclusion
5. Organizational structure

Career Checkup Exercises

Take time to complete these exercises

1. Career Satisfaction Survey
2. Skills Matrix
3. Work-Life Balance Wheel
4. Career Advancement Roadmap
5. Company Culture Assessment
6. Compensation and Benefits Analysis
7. Professional Development Plan

Interpreting Your Results

1. Identify areas of strength and weakness

2. Prioritize improvements

3. Develop a plan for addressing weaknesses

4. Celebrate successes

Tools for Conducting a Career Checkup

- **Self-Assessment Questionnaires:** Use tools like SWOT analysis (Strengths, Weaknesses, Opportunities, Threats) to evaluate your current position.

- **Career Counselling:** Engage with a career coach or counsellor for expert guidance.

- **Skill Assessments:** Platforms like LinkedIn Learning or Coursera can help identify skill gaps.

- **Feedback Mechanisms:** Regular performance reviews and peer feedback sessions can provide clarity.

What to Do After Your Career Checkup

1. Celebrate What's Working

2. If your career checkup reveals that you're on the right track, take a moment to celebrate your successes and continue building on them.

3. **Address Weaknesses**

4. Identify areas that need improvement. For example:

   - If skill gaps exist, enrol in training or certification programs.

   - If you lack growth opportunities, consider discussing potential projects or promotions with your manager.

5. Consider a Career Pivot

6. If your checkup reveals dissatisfaction or misalignment, explore options for a career change. This might involve:

- Switching roles within your current organization.

- Exploring opportunities in a new field.

- Starting your own business or freelancing.

7. **Set Actionable Goals**

8. Based on your findings, create a clear action plan with short- and long-term goals. For example:

   - Short-term: Attend industry networking events.

   - Long-term: Transition into a leadership role within two years.

Real-Life Examples

Meet Emily, who realized her job satisfaction was low due to lack of autonomy:

"I'm transitioning to a freelance writing career to gain flexibility."

Or David, who discovered his skills were underutilized:

"I'm pursuing a certification program to enhance my data analysis skills."

Common Challenges and Solutions

1. Lack of challenge: Seek new responsibilities or projects.

2. Poor work-life balance: Establish boundaries and prioritize self-care.

3. Limited career advancement: Seek mentorship or training.

Call to Action

It's time to take control of your career! Schedule your career checkup today, reflect on where you are, and map out where you want to be. Whether you need to refine your current path or embark on a new one, a thoughtful evaluation can set the stage for a brighter and more fulfilling future.

Conclusion

Your Career Checkup provides valuable insights into your current career. By evaluating your job satisfaction, skills utilization, work-life balance, career advancement, company culture, compensation, and professional development, you'll make informed decisions about your next steps.

In the next chapter, we'll explore exploring new career options and identifying potential paths.

Reflection Exercise

1. What areas of your current career need improvement?

2. How aligned is your current role with your career purpose?

3. What skills or knowledge gaps need addressing?

Action Plan

1. Schedule time for self-reflection.

2. Research resources for skill development and career advancement.

3. Develop a plan to address weaknesses.

By conducting your Career Checkup, you'll take the first step toward transforming your career and elevating your life.

Additional Resources

1. "The 4-Hour Work Week" by Timothy Ferriss

2. "StrengthsFinder" by Tom Rath

3. "The Career Coaching Group" online resources

4. "LinkedIn Learning" courses

5. "Glassdoor" salary and company reviews

4

Exploring New Horizons - Discovering Alternative Career Paths

In Chapter 3, we conducted a Career Checkup, evaluating your current path and identifying areas for improvement. Now, we'll explore alternative career paths, discovering new horizons that align with your passions, skills, and values.

In a rapidly changing world, the concept of a single, lifelong career is becoming outdated. Whether you're seeking growth, facing industry shifts, or simply yearning for something new, exploring alternative career paths can open doors to exciting opportunities. This chapter will guide you through the process of identifying, evaluating, and transitioning into alternative careers that align with your skills, passions, and values.

Why Explore Alternative Career Paths?

1. Enhance job satisfaction and engagement
2. Leverage transferable skills
3. Align with your career purpose
4. Increase earning potential
5. Expand professional network
6. Develop new skills and expertise
7. Improve work-life balance
8. Reduce stress and burnout
9. Increase personal fulfilment
10. Stay relevant in a changing job market

Identifying Alternative Career Paths

Consider

1. Industry shifts: Transition to a new industry
2. Functional changes: Switch roles within the same industry
3. Entrepreneurial ventures: Start your own business
4. Freelance or consulting: Offer services on a project basis
5. Non-profit or social impact: Make a difference in your community
6. Online or remote work: Explore flexible work arrangements
7. Creative or artistic pursuits: Monetize your hobbies
8. Education or training: Share your expertise

Exploring Emerging Industries

1. Renewable energy and sustainability
2. Healthcare technology and biotech
3. Artificial intelligence and machine learning
4. Cybersecurity and data protection
5. Creative industries and digital media
6. E-commerce and digital marketing
7. Environmental Conservation
8. Social entrepreneurship

Assessing Alternative Career Paths

Evaluate

1. Alignment with your values and passions
2. Transferable skills and expertise
3. Growth opportunities and advancement
4. Compensation and benefits
5. Work-life balance and flexibility
6. Industry outlook and job security
7. Required education and training
8. Networking opportunities
9. Personal fulfilment
10. Cultural fit

Categorizing Alternative Career Paths

1. Linear Career Progression: Advancement within your current industry
2. Career Pivot: Transition to a related industry or role

3. Career Transformation: Complete career change

4. Entrepreneurial Venture: Starting your own business

Career Exploration Tools

Utilize

1. LinkedIn's Job Explorer: Research job titles and companies

2. Glassdoor: Review company culture and salaries

3. Career Assessments: Identify strengths and interests

4. Networking Events: Connect with professionals in your desired field

5. Informational Interviews: Learn from industry experts

6. Job Shadowing: Experience a day in the life

Steps to Transition to a New Career

1. **Start Small**

    Explore your chosen field through freelance projects, internships, or volunteering. This allows you to gain hands-on experience without a full commitment.

2. **Upskill**

    Enrol in courses, attend workshops, or earn certifications relevant to your new career. Platforms like Coursera, Udemy, and LinkedIn Learning offer flexible learning options.

3. **Leverage Your Network**

    Inform your professional network about your career transition. Connections often lead to opportunities or valuable advice.

4. **Tailor Your Resume and LinkedIn Profile**

    Highlight transferable skills and relevant experiences that showcase your suitability for the new role.

5. Stay Persistent

   Transitioning careers may take time. Be patient, persistent, and open to learning from challenges along the way.

Why People Explore Alternative Career Paths

Several triggers can inspire someone to seek a new professional direction:

- **Burnout:** A high-stress job with no room for personal growth or work-life balance.

- **Desire for Impact:** Wanting to contribute meaningfully to society or a cause.

- **Financial Stability:** Exploring careers with higher earning potential or better financial prospects.

- **Life Changes:** Shifts in personal circumstances, like becoming a parent or relocating, which might demand more flexibility or a fresh start.

- **Curiosity and Growth:** A natural desire to learn new skills and expand horizons.

Steps to Transition to an Alternative Career Path

1. **Test the Waters**

   Start with small steps. Freelance, volunteer, or take on side projects in the new field to gain practical experience.

2. **Invest in Education and Training**

   Enrol in courses, attend workshops, or pursue certifications relevant to your chosen career. Online platforms like Coursera, Udemy, and LinkedIn Learning offer flexible options.

3. **Network with Experts**

   Reach out to professionals in your desired field for mentorship and advice. Building relationships can provide valuable insights and open doors.

4. **Redesign Your Resume and Online Presence**

   Highlight transferable skills and relevant experiences on your resume and LinkedIn profile. Showcase how your background aligns with the requirements of the new career.

5. **Be Open to Entry-Level Roles**

   Starting fresh might mean taking a step back to learn and grow. Use this opportunity to build credibility in your new field.

The Joy of Exploring New Horizons

Transitioning to an alternative career path can be an enriching journey that brings:

- Renewed energy and enthusiasm for work.

- Opportunities to learn and grow in new ways.

- A sense of purpose that aligns with your personal values.

Real-Life Examples

Meet Sarah, who transitioned from finance to environmental sustainability:

"I'm now working as a sustainability consultant, aligning my career with my passion for the environment."

Or John, who shifted from marketing to software development:

"I'm loving my new role as a developer, leveraging my creativity and problem-solving skills."

Overcoming Obstacles

1. Fear of uncertainty: Research and plan carefully

2. Lack of experience: Pursue training and certifications

3. Networking challenges: Attend industry events

4. Self-doubt: Focus on transferable skills and strengths

5. Financial constraints: Explore cost-effective education options

Action Plan

1. Research alternative career paths
2. Network with professionals in your desired field
3. Update your skills and expertise
4. Create a transition plan
5. Take calculated risks
6. Seek mentorship
7. Join industry groups

Overcoming Fear of Change

Fear of failure, uncertainty, or judgment often keeps people from exploring alternative paths. To overcome these fears:

- Focus on possibilities rather than limitations.

- Break the transition into small, manageable steps.

- Seek support from mentors, career coaches, or peers who've made similar changes.

The Benefits of Exploring New Horizons

- **Personal Growth:** Learning new skills and stepping out of your comfort zone fosters confidence and resilience.

- **Career Satisfaction:** Aligning your work with your passions leads to a more fulfilling career.

- **Broader Perspectives:** Exposure to diverse fields and industries enriches your understanding and adaptability.

Call to Action

Your dream career might be just around the corner—are you ready to explore it? Take the first step today: reflect on your interests, research new opportunities, and start planning your journey. The possibilities are endless, and the rewards can be life-changing.

Start now, and discover a career that not only supports your livelihood but also fuels your passion and purpose!

Conclusion

Exploring alternative career paths opens doors to new opportunities, aligning your career with your passions, skills, and values. By identifying emerging industries, assessing alternative paths, and utilizing career exploration tools, you'll make informed decisions about your future.

In the next chapter, we'll discuss building a strong professional network, essential for career advancement.

Reflection Exercise

1. What alternative career paths align with your values and passions?

2. What skills and expertise do you need to acquire?

3. What obstacles might you face, and how will you overcome them?

Additional Resources

1. "What Colour is Your Parachute?" by Richard N. Bolles

2. "The Start-Up of You: Adapt to the Future, Invest in Yourself, and Transform Your Career" by Reid Hoffman

3. "Pivot: The Art and Science of Reinventing Your Career and Life" by Jenny Blake

<h1 style="text-align:center">5</h1>

Building a Strong Professional Network - The Key to Career Advancement

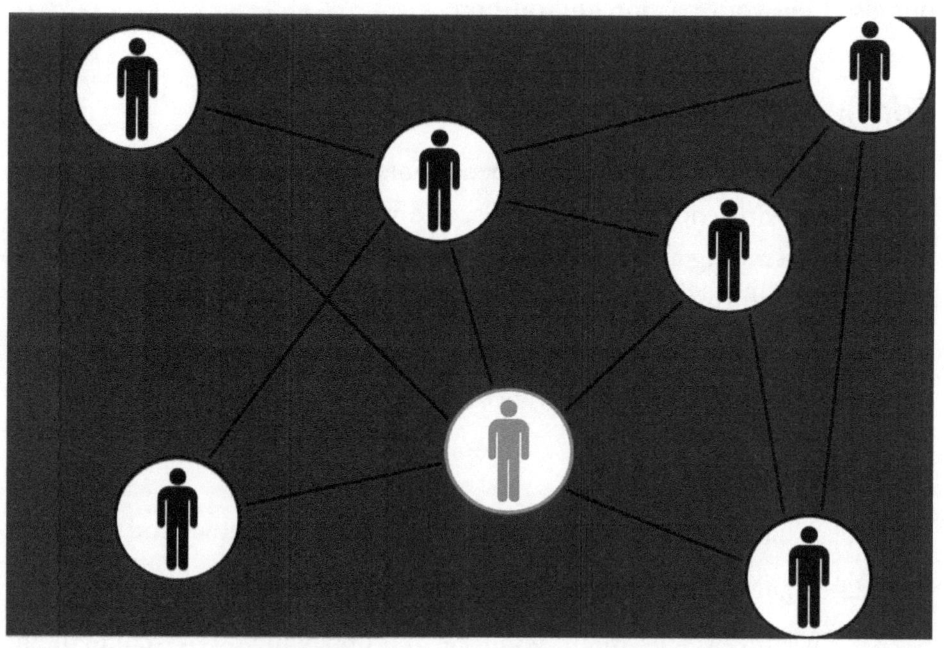

In Chapter 4, we explored alternative career paths, discovering new horizons that align with your passions, skills, and values. Now, we'll focus on building a strong professional network, which is essential for career advancement.

In today's interconnected world, a strong professional network is one of the most powerful tools for career success. While your skills, experience, and qualifications are essential, the relationships you build with others often play an equally significant role in advancing your career. A robust network opens doors to new opportunities, provides mentorship, and enhances your visibility in your industry. This chapter will guide you on how to cultivate, grow, and leverage your professional network effectively.

Why Networking Matters for Career Growth

Networking isn't just about meeting people—it's about building genuine relationships that are mutually beneficial. Here's why it's critical for career advancement:

1. **Access to Opportunities:** Many jobs and opportunities aren't publicly advertised but are filled through personal referrals or insider recommendations.

2. **Mentorship and Guidance:** Networking connects you with experienced professionals who can offer advice, mentorship, and support as you navigate your career path.

3. **Skill Enhancement:** Interacting with peers and industry leaders allows you to learn new skills and stay updated on industry trends.

4. **Visibility:** A strong network increases your presence and credibility within your professional community.

5. **Support System:** Your network can provide encouragement and resources during career transitions or challenging times.

Steps to Build a Strong Professional Network

1. Start with a Foundation of Authenticity

   Networking is most effective when it's genuine. Focus on building meaningful relationships rather than simply collecting contacts.

Approach networking with the mindset of giving as much as you hope to gain.

2. **Leverage Existing Connections**

Begin with the people you already know—colleagues, classmates, friends, and family. Strengthen these relationships by staying in touch, offering help, and expressing gratitude for their support.

3. **Attend Networking Events**

Participate in conferences, workshops, seminars, and industry meetups. These events provide an excellent opportunity to meet professionals in your field and broaden your network.

4. **Utilize Online Platforms**

Platforms like LinkedIn are invaluable for networking.

- **Optimize Your Profile:** Make sure your LinkedIn profile is complete and professional, highlighting your skills, achievements, and aspirations.

- **Join Groups:** Participate in LinkedIn groups relevant to your industry or interests to engage in discussions and connect with like-minded individuals.

- **Share Content:** Post articles, insights, and updates to demonstrate your expertise and keep your profile active.

5. **Seek Out Mentors and Sponsors**

A mentor provides guidance and advice, while a sponsor actively advocates for your career growth. Identify and connect with individuals who can play these roles in your professional journey.

6. **Be Proactive in Reaching Out**

Don't wait for others to approach you—take the initiative to introduce yourself to new contacts. A well-crafted email or a thoughtful LinkedIn message can go a long way in starting a relationship.

Networking Do's and Don'ts

Do's

- **Be Authentic:** People appreciate sincerity and a genuine interest in building relationships.

- **Follow Up:** After meeting someone, send a thank-you note or connect on LinkedIn to maintain the relationship.

- **Be a Giver:** Offer value to your network, whether it's sharing knowledge, introducing contacts, or helping with a project.

- **Stay Consistent:** Regularly engage with your network through check-ins, updates, and attending events.

Don'ts

- **Avoid Being Transactional:** Networking isn't just about what others can do for you. Focus on building two-way relationships.

- **Don't Neglect Your Network:** Maintaining relationships requires consistent effort—don't let connections fade over time.

- **Avoid Overwhelming Requests:** Be respectful of others' time and avoid making excessive demands.

How to Strengthen and Maintain Your Network

1. **Stay in Touch**

   Regularly connect with your contacts through messages, calls, or meetings. Share updates about your career and inquire about theirs.

2. **Engage on Social Media**

   Like, comment, and share content from your professional connections on platforms like LinkedIn. This keeps you visible and engaged.

3. **Attend Reunions and Gatherings**

   Reconnecting with old colleagues, classmates, or friends at alumni events or industry gatherings can reignite valuable relationships.

4. **Show Gratitude**

   Express appreciation for any support or opportunities provided by your network. A simple thank-you note can leave a lasting impression.

5. **Offer Help**

   Always look for ways to give back to your network. Helping others strengthens relationships and builds goodwill.

Leveraging Your Network for Career Advancement

1. **Seek Job Referrals**

   If you're job hunting, reach out to your network for referrals and insights about potential openings.

2. **Gain Industry Insights**

   Use your network to stay informed about trends, challenges, and opportunities in your field.

3. **Find Collaborators**

   Whether you're starting a new project or business, your network can connect you with partners, investors, or team members.

4. **Access Mentorship**

   Tap into the experience of your contacts to gain advice on navigating career challenges or achieving goals.

5. **Expand Influence**

   Speaking engagements, collaborations, or co-authoring articles with network members can increase your professional visibility.

Real-Life Networking Success Stories

1. **From Internship to Dream Job**

   During a college internship, Jane connected with her manager on LinkedIn. Years later, when she was job hunting, that connection referred her to a position, landing her a dream job.

2. **The Entrepreneurial Collaboration**

   Raj met his future co-founder at a tech meetup. Their shared interests and complementary skills led to the creation of a successful startup.

3. **The Mentor's Guidance**

   Alex's mentor introduced him to a senior executive in their industry, which eventually led to a leadership role in a Fortune 500 company.

These examples highlight how networking can have a profound impact on career trajectories.

Overcoming Networking Challenges

1. **Introversion**

   If you're shy or introverted, focus on one-on-one interactions and online networking, which may feel less intimidating.

2. **Time Constraints**

   Dedicate a few hours each month to networking activities, such as attending an event or reaching out to contacts.

3. **Fear of Rejection**

   Not everyone will respond positively, and that's okay. Focus on building relationships with those who show interest.

The Long-Term Benefits of Networking

A strong professional network is an investment in your career. It not only helps you achieve immediate goals but also provides a lifelong support system as you navigate various stages of your professional journey.

Why Build a Professional Network?

1. Access valuable information and resources
2. Increase job opportunities and referrals
3. Enhance career visibility and credibility
4. Develop meaningful relationships and mentorship
5. Stay updated on industry trends and news
6. Expand your skill set through collaborations
7. Gain access to exclusive events and opportunities
8. Improve your negotiation skills and confidence
9. Enhance personal growth and development
10. Increase earning potential

Understanding Networking Types

1. Informal Networking: Casual conversations and connections
2. Formal Networking: Structured events and organizations
3. Online Networking: social media and digital platforms
4. Strategic Networking: Targeted connections and partnerships
5. Internal Networking: Building relationships within your organization

Building Your Professional Network

Step 1: Identify Your Goals and Objectives

1. Define your career aspirations

2. Determine your networking needs

3. Research industry events and conferences

Step 2: Research and Join Professional Associations

1. Industry-specific organizations

2. Local business networks

3. Alumni associations

4. Online communities and forums

Step 3: Attend Networking Events

1. Conferences and seminars

2. Networking meetings and sessions

3. Industry-specific events

4. Volunteer opportunities

Step 4: Engage in Online Communities

1. LinkedIn: Connect with professionals and join groups

2. Twitter: Engage in industry conversations and hashtags

3. Facebook: Join professional groups and events

4. Instagram: Showcase your skills and expertise

Step 5: Develop a Strong Elevator Pitch

1. Clearly articulate your value proposition

2. Highlight your skills and expertise

3. Showcase your achievements

Effective Networking Strategies

1. Practice active listening and engagement
2. Ask thoughtful and relevant questions
3. Show genuine interest and curiosity
4. Follow up and follow through
5. Be proactive and take initiative
6. Offer value and expertise
7. Build relationships, not just connections
8. Leverage your network for introductions

Utilizing Social Media for Networking

LinkedIn

1. Optimize your profile
2. Connect with professionals
3. Join industry-specific groups

X(Formerly Twitter)

1. Engage in industry conversations
2. Use relevant hashtags
3. Follow industry leaders

Facebook

1. Join professional groups
2. Attend online events
3. Connect with colleagues and peers

Real-Life Examples

Meet Emily, who landed her dream job through networking:

"I connected with an industry leader on LinkedIn, and she introduced me to the hiring manager."

Or David, who found a business partner through networking:

"I met my co-founder at a startup event, and we launched a successful company together."

Overcoming Networking Challenges

1. Shyness or introversion: Prepare and practice beforehand
2. Time constraints: Prioritize and focus on key events
3. Rejection or disappointment: Persist and stay positive
4. Self-promotion: Focus on providing value and expertise
5. Networking fatigue: Take breaks and recharge

Action Plan

1. Set networking goals and objectives
2. Research and attend industry events
3. Join professional associations and groups
4. Engage in online communities and forums
5. Develop a strong elevator pitch
6. Practice active listening and engagement
7. Follow up and follow through

Call to Action

Start building your professional network today! Reach out to old connections, attend an industry event, or send a thoughtful message to someone you admire. Every new connection is a step toward a stronger, more successful career. Remember, the key to networking is authenticity, consistency, and a willingness to give as much as you receive.

Your future opportunities may just be a conversation away—take that step now!

Conclusion

Building a strong professional network is crucial for career advancement. By understanding networking types, building your network, and utilizing effective strategies, you'll access valuable resources, increase job opportunities, and enhance your career visibility.

In the next chapter, we'll discuss developing a personal brand, which is essential for standing out in a competitive job market.

Reflection Exercise

1. What are your networking goals and objectives?

2. Who are the key people you want to connect with?

3. What events and groups will you attend?

Additional Resources

1. "Networking Like a Pro" by Brian Hilliard and Ivan Misner

2. "The Networking Survival Guide" by Diane Darling

3. "How to Work a Room" by Susan Rothenberg

4. "LinkedIn's Networking Guide" by LinkedIn Learning

5. "Networking for People Who Hate Networking" by Nancy Ancowitz

Part 2

Building Foundations for Success

6

Developing a Strong Personal Brand - Stand Out in a Competitive Job Market

"Your personal brand is what sets you apart from others."

– Gary Vaynerchuk

In Chapter 5, we discussed building a strong professional network, which is essential for career advancement. Now, we'll focus on developing a strong personal brand, crucial for standing out in a competitive job market.

By building a compelling personal brand, you can make a lasting impression on employers, clients, and colleagues, ensuring that you stand out from the competition.

What is a Personal Brand?

A personal brand is the perception people have of you professionally. It's shaped by:

- **Your Expertise:** Your skills, qualifications, and achievements.

- **Your Personality:** How you interact with others and approach challenges.

- **Your Values:** The principles and beliefs that guide your decisions.

- **Your Unique Selling Proposition (USP):** What makes you different from others in your field?

A strong personal brand communicates your value clearly and consistently, positioning you as a credible and trustworthy professional.

Why is Personal Branding Important?

1. **Differentiation**

   In a competitive market, a personal brand helps you stand out from other candidates with similar qualifications.

2. **Credibility and Trust**

   A well-crafted personal brand establishes your expertise and builds trust among peers, employers, and clients.

3. **Career Advancement**

   Your personal brand can open doors to new opportunities, including job offers, promotions, and collaborations.

4. **Networking Power**

   A recognizable and memorable personal brand makes it easier to connect with like-minded professionals and grow your network.

5. **Control Over Your Narrative**

   By intentionally shaping your personal brand, you ensure that others perceive you the way you want to be seen.

Steps to Develop a Strong Personal Brand

1. **Define Your Unique Value Proposition**

   Start by identifying what makes you unique. Ask yourself:

   - What skills or experiences set me apart?

   - What am I passionate about in my field?

   - What problems can I solve better than others?

   Your unique value proposition is the foundation of your personal brand. For example, if you're a digital marketer, your USP might be your expertise in creating data-driven campaigns that deliver measurable results.

2. **Identify Your Target Audience**

   Determine who you want to influence with your brand. This could include:

   - Hiring managers and recruiters.

   - Industry peers and thought leaders.

   - Potential clients or collaborators.

Tailor your messaging and approach to resonate with this audience.

1. **Craft a Personal Brand Statement**

   Create a concise and impactful statement that summarizes who you are, what you do, and what you stand for. For example:

   - "I'm a UX designer passionate about creating intuitive digital experiences that connect brands with their audiences."

2. **Optimize Your Online Presence**

3. In the digital age, your online presence is a critical part of your personal brand.

   - **LinkedIn:** Ensure your profile is complete, with a professional photo, a compelling headline, and detailed descriptions of your experiences and achievements.

   - **Social media:** Use platforms like Twitter, Instagram, or Medium to share insights, achievements, and industry-related content.

   - **Portfolio:** If applicable, create an online portfolio to showcase your work.

4. **Consistently Share Value**

   Establish yourself as an expert by consistently sharing valuable content:

   - Write blog posts or articles about your industry.

   - Share insights or lessons learned from your experiences.

   - Engage with and comment on posts from others in your field.

5. **Network Strategically**

   Attend industry events, participate in webinars, and engage with professional groups to build relationships that reinforce your personal brand.

6. **Seek Feedback**

   Regularly ask colleagues, mentors, and peers for feedback on how you're perceived. Use this input to refine your personal brand.

7. **Be Authentic**

   Authenticity is key to building trust. Stay true to your values and personality, and avoid trying to imitate someone else's brand.

Common Mistakes to Avoid

1. **Inconsistency**

   Your personal brand should be cohesive across all platforms and interactions. Mixed messages can confuse your audience.

2. **Over-Emphasizing Yourself**

   While promoting yourself is important, focus on how you can add value to others.

3. **Neglecting Your Online Reputation**

   Employers and clients often Google potential hires or partners. Ensure your online presence is professional and aligns with your personal brand.

4. **Failing to Evolve**

   Your personal brand should grow as you gain new experiences and skills. Regularly update your brand to reflect your professional journey.

The Role of Storytelling in Personal Branding

Humans connect with stories. Use storytelling to make your personal brand relatable and memorable.

- Share your journey: Highlight pivotal moments that shaped your career.

- Showcase challenges: Discuss obstacles you've overcome and what you learned.

- Celebrate achievements: Talk about successes, big or small, to demonstrate your growth.

For instance, if you transitioned from being a teacher to a corporate trainer, sharing that story can make your brand more compelling.

Real-Life Examples of Strong Personal Brands

1. **The Thought Leader**

   A software engineer writes insightful LinkedIn posts about emerging technologies, contributing to industry discussions. As a result, they're invited to speak at conferences and gain visibility as a thought leader.

2. **The Niche Expert**

   A marketing professional focuses on e-commerce strategies, creating blog posts, videos, and case studies. Their specialized knowledge attracts clients looking for e-commerce expertise.

3. **The Authentic Storyteller**

   A career coach shares personal experiences about overcoming setbacks, making them relatable and trustworthy to their audience.

These examples demonstrate how intentional branding can lead to recognition and opportunities.

Maintaining and Growing Your Personal Brand

1. **Stay Relevant**

   Regularly update your skills and knowledge to ensure your personal brand reflects current trends and expertise.

2. **Engage with Your Audience**

   Respond to comments, participate in discussions, and acknowledge feedback to strengthen your connections.

3. **Monitor Your Brand**

   Use tools like Google Alerts to stay informed about how your name and brand are being mentioned online.

4. **Be Patient**

   Building a strong personal brand takes time. Stay consistent and committed to your goals.

Why Develop a **Personal Brand?**

1. Differentiate yourself from others
2. Establish credibility and expertise
3. Increase visibility and recognition
4. Enhance career opportunities and advancement
5. Build trust and loyalty with your audience
6. Increase earning potential
7. Improve self-confidence and self-awareness
8. Enhance online presence and digital footprint
9. Foster meaningful relationships and collaborations
10. Stay relevant in a rapidly changing job market

Understanding Personal Branding

1. Define your unique value proposition (UVP)
2. Identify your target audience
3. Develop a consistent message and image
4. Establish a strong online presence
5. Showcase your skills and expertise
6. Engage with your audience and build relationships
7. Continuously evaluate and improve your brand

Creating Your Personal Brand Statement

1. Define your passions and values
2. Identify your strengths and skills
3. Determine your career goals
4. Craft a compelling brand statement
5. Consider your personal mission statement

Elements of a Strong Personal Brand

1. Visual Identity: Logo, colour scheme, typography
2. Tone and Voice: Authentic, consistent communication
3. Personal Story: Share your experiences and lessons learned
4. Expertise: Showcase your skills and knowledge
5. Values: Align with your audience's values
6. Uniqueness: Differentiate yourself from others
7. Consistency: Maintain a cohesive brand image

Building Your Online Presence

1. Website or Blog: Establish a professional hub
2. Social media: Leverage platforms for visibility
3. LinkedIn: Optimize your profile and engage
4. Personal Email: Create a professional address
5. Video Content: Showcase your personality and skills

Content Creation and Curation

1. Blogging: Share your expertise and experiences
2. Video Content: Showcase your personality and skills
3. Podcasting: Engage with your audience and industry leaders
4. Social Media Posts: Share valuable insights and news
5. Guest Blogging: Expand your audience and credibility

Collaborative Tools for Personal Branding

1. Canva: Visual design and branding
2. WordPress: Website and blog creation
3. Hootsuite: Social media management
4. LinkedIn Learning: Skill development and training
5. Calendly: Scheduling and meeting management

Overcoming Personal Branding Challenges

1. Self-doubt: Focus on your strengths and accomplishments
2. Lack of clarity: Define your UVP (unique value proposition) and brand statement
3. Time constraints: Prioritize and focus on key platforms
4. Authenticity: Be true to yourself and your values
5. Feedback: Encourage constructive criticism

Action Plan

1. Define your personal brand statement
2. Establish a strong online presence
3. Create and curate valuable content
4. Engage with your audience and build relationships
5. Continuously evaluate and improve your brand
6. Collaborate with others to expand your reach

The Impact of a Strong Personal Brand

A well-developed personal brand doesn't just help you land a job—it positions you as a leader in your field. It attracts opportunities, fosters trust, and sets you up for long-term success.

Call to Action

Your personal brand is your professional signature—make it count! Start today by defining your unique value, refining your online presence, and sharing your expertise. Remember, your brand is a reflection of who you are and the value you bring to the world. Stand out, shine brightly, and let your brand speak for you in every opportunity.

Conclusion

Developing a strong personal brand is crucial for standing out in a competitive job market. By understanding personal branding, creating a personal brand statement, and building your online presence, you'll establish credibility, increase visibility, and enhance career opportunities.

In the next chapter, we'll discuss negotiating salary and benefits, essential for maximizing your earning potential.

Reflection Exercise

1. What are your personal brand's core values and message?

2. Who is your target audience?

3. What platforms will you use to establish your online presence?

Additional Resources

1. "Personal Branding for Dummies" by Susan Chritton

2. "Crushing It!" by Gary Vaynerchuk

3. "The Personal Branding Blueprint" by Josh Turner

4. "Influencer: The Power to Change Anything" by Joseph Grenny

7

Negotiating Salary and Benefits - Maximize Your Earning Potential

"*Negotiation is not about getting everything you want; it's about getting what you need.*"

– Josh Weiss

In Chapter 6, we discussed developing a strong personal brand, crucial for standing out in a competitive job market. Now, we'll focus on negotiating salary and benefits, essential for maximizing your earning potential.

Negotiating salary and benefits is one of the most critical yet underutilized skills in the professional world. Whether you're starting a new job or seeking a raise in your current role, effective negotiation ensures you're compensated fairly for your skills, experience, and contributions. This chapter will explore strategies, tips, and insights to help you confidently navigate salary discussions and maximize your earning potential.

Negotiating salary and benefits is one of the most critical yet underutilized skills in the professional world. Whether you're starting a new job or seeking a raise in your current role, effective negotiation ensures you're compensated fairly for your skills, experience, and contributions. This chapter will explore strategies, tips, and insights to help you confidently navigate salary discussions and maximize your earning potential.

Why Negotiation Matters

1. **Reflects Your Value**

   Negotiating demonstrates that you understand your worth in the marketplace.

2. **Builds Financial Security**

   Even a small increase in salary can have a significant long-term impact on your earnings and savings.

3. **Sets the Tone**

   Negotiating during the job offer stage establishes expectations for how your value will be recognized in the future.

4. **Improves Benefits Beyond Salary**

   Compensation isn't just about money; it includes benefits, bonuses, and other perks that enhance your overall package.

Preparing for Salary Negotiation

1. **Research Market Rates**

   - Use resources like Glassdoor, PayScale, and industry reports to determine the typical salary range for your role, location, and experience level.

- Talk to peers in your field to gain insights into current compensation trends.

2. **Know Your Value**

   - List your skills, achievements, and unique qualifications that set you apart.

   - Quantify your contributions wherever possible (e.g., "Increased sales by 20%," "Reduced project timelines by 15%").

3. **Set Your Salary Range**

   - Determine your target salary, a comfortable minimum, and an ambitious but realistic upper limit.

   - Be prepared to justify your range with data and examples.

4. **Understand the Full Compensation Package**

   - Consider other benefits that add value, such as health insurance, retirement plans, bonuses, stock options, vacation time, and flexible work arrangements.

   - Decide which benefits are most important to you.

5. **Practice Your Pitch**

   - Rehearse your negotiation with a trusted friend or mentor.

   - Anticipate possible objections and prepare responses.

The Art of Salary Negotiation

1. **Choose the Right Time**

   - For new jobs, negotiate after receiving the offer but before accepting it.

   - For raises, request a meeting during performance reviews or after completing a significant achievement.

2. **Start the Conversation Confidently**

   - Express enthusiasm for the role or company while stating your desire to discuss compensation.

- Example: "I'm excited about this opportunity and would like to discuss how we can align the compensation with my experience and the industry standard."

3. **Present Your Case**

   - Highlight your achievements, skills, and the value you bring to the organization.

   - Use phrases like:

   - "Based on my research and industry benchmarks…"

   - "Given my experience in [specific skill/achievement] …"

4. **Use Anchoring Effectively**

   - Start with a salary slightly above your target to leave room for negotiation.

Be Flexible but Firm

- Be open to compromise on non-monetary benefits if the salary cannot meet your expectations.

- Example: "If the salary is fixed, could we explore additional vacation days or professional development opportunities?"

Stay Calm and Professional

- Avoid emotional appeals; focus on facts and your professional value.

- Remain courteous even if the negotiation doesn't go as planned.

Negotiating Benefits Beyond Salary

Sometimes, employers may have limited flexibility with base salary but can offer other valuable perks:

- **Bonuses and Incentives:** *Annual, performance-based, or signing bonuses.*

- **Health and Wellness Benefits:** *Better health coverage, gym memberships, or wellness programs.*

- **Professional Development:** *Opportunities for training, certifications, or attending conferences.*

- **Work-Life Balance:** *Flexible schedules, remote work options, or additional paid time off.*

- **Stock Options or Equity:** *Particularly relevant in startups or growing companies.*

Common Mistakes to Avoid

1. Accepting the First Offer:

   Employers often expect you to negotiate, so don't settle for the initial offer without discussion.

2. Lack of Preparation:

   Going into a negotiation without knowing your worth or market trends weakens your position.

3. Focusing Solely on Salary:

   Overlooking benefits and perks can mean leaving value on the table.

4. **Being Overly Aggressive**

5. Pushy or confrontational behaviour can harm your relationship with the employer.

   Not Getting It in Writing

6. Ensure all agreed terms are documented in your offer letter or employment contract.

What to Do if the Employer Says No

1. **Ask for Feedback**

   If your request is declined, inquire politely about the decision.

   - Example: "Could you share more about the budget constraints or how we might revisit this conversation in the future?"

2. **Explore Other Options**

   Negotiate for non-salary benefits or agree to revisit the discussion after a specific period.

3. **Evaluate the Offer**

   Consider the entire package, company culture, and growth opportunities before making a decision.

4. **Know When to Walk Away**

5. If the offer doesn't meet your needs and flexibility is limited, it's okay to decline and seek opportunities elsewhere.

Key Takeaways for Effective Negotiation

1. **Do Your Homework:** Research is the cornerstone of a successful negotiation.

2. **Be Confident but Respectful:** Assert your value while maintaining professionalism.

Why Negotiate Salary and Benefits?

1. Increase earning potential

2. Improve job satisfaction

3. Enhance benefits and perks

4. Demonstrate self-worth and confidence

5. Set a strong foundation for future negotiations

6. Align compensation with industry standards

7. Consider long-term financial goals

8. Enhance work-life balance

9. Secure professional development opportunities

10. Build a stronger employer-employee relationship

Understanding Salary Negotiation

1. Research industry standards and market rates
2. Evaluate job requirements and responsibilities
3. Assess your skills, experience, and achievements
4. Determine your minimum acceptable salary
5. Develop a negotiation strategy
6. Consider cost of living adjustments
7. Factor in bonuses and incentives
8. Evaluate stock options and equity

Salary Negotiation Strategies

1. Know your worth: Confidently articulate your value
2. Do your research: Understand market rates and industry standards
3. Be flexible: Consider alternative compensation options
4. Be respectful: Maintain a professional tone
5. Be prepared: Anticipate common negotiation questions
6. Use silence effectively
7. Avoid emotional decisions
8. Leverage competing offers

Benefit Negotiation

1. Health insurance and wellness programs
2. Retirement plans and pension schemes
3. Paid time off and vacation days
4. Professional development opportunities
5. Flexible work arrangements and remote work
6. Stock options and equity
7. Signing bonuses and relocation assistance

8. Childcare and education benefits

9. Commuter benefits and transportation reimbursement

10. Employee assistance programs

Real-Life Examples

Meet Emily, who successfully negotiated her salary:

"I researched industry standards and confidently articulated my value, resulting in a 20% salary increase."

Or David, who negotiated flexible work arrangements:

"I requested remote work options and flexible hours, improving my work-life balance."

Common Negotiation Mistakes

1. Lack of research and preparation

2. Fear of rejection or confrontation

3. Unrealistic expectations

4. Failure to articulate value

5. Inadequate communication

6. Lack of flexibility

7. Insufficient leverage

8. Emotional decision-making

Overcoming Negotiation Challenges

1. Build confidence: Focus on your strengths and achievements

2. Stay calm: Manage negotiation anxiety

3. Seek support: Consult mentors or career coaches

4. Be open-minded: Consider alternative options

5. Practice active listening: Understand employer needs

6. Develop a growth mindset

7. Prepare for common objections

8. Maintain a positive attitude

Action Plan

1. Research industry standards and market rates

2. Evaluate job requirements and responsibilities

3. Develop a negotiation strategy

4. Practice confident communication

5. Consider alternative compensation options

6. Review and revise your negotiation approach

7. Prepare for common negotiation questions

8. Seek support from mentors or career coaches

Conclusion

Negotiating salary and benefits is crucial for maximizing your earning potential. By understanding salary negotiation, developing effective strategies, and avoiding common mistakes, you'll confidently articulate your worth and secure a fair compensation package.

In the next chapter, we'll discuss managing conflict and difficult conversations, essential for maintaining a positive work environment.

Reflection Exercise

1. What are your salary and benefit expectations?

2. How will you articulate your value and worth?

3. What negotiation strategies will you employ?

4. What benefits are most important to you?

5. How will you handle common negotiation challenges?

Additional Resources

1. "Negotiating Your Salary" by Jack Chapman
2. "The Negotiation Book" by Steve Gates
3. "Getting to Yes" by Roger Fisher and William Ury
4. "Crucial Conversations" by Kerry Patterson
5. "Influence: The Psychology of Persuasion" by Robert Cialdini
6. "The Art of Possibility" by Rosamund Stone Zander and Benjamin Zander
7. "Negotiation Genius" by Deepak Malhotra

8

Managing Conflict and Difficult Conversations - Essential Skills for Success

In Chapter 7, we discussed negotiating salary and benefits, crucial for maximizing your earning potential. Now, we'll focus on managing conflict and difficult conversations, essential skills for maintaining a positive work environment.

Conflict is an inevitable part of professional and personal life. Whether it arises from differences in opinions, misunderstandings, or competing interests, the ability to navigate conflict effectively is a critical skill. Similarly, handling difficult conversations—whether giving constructive feedback, addressing performance issues, or discussing sensitive topics—requires tact, empathy, and clear communication. This chapter explores strategies for managing conflict and conducting challenging discussions to foster understanding, collaboration, and positive outcomes.

Understanding the Nature of Conflict

Conflict occurs when two or more parties perceive their goals, needs, or values as being at odds. While often seen as negative, conflict can also lead to growth and innovation if managed constructively.

Common Causes of Conflict in the Workplace

1. **Communication Gaps:** Misunderstandings due to unclear or incomplete communication.

2. **Personality Clashes:** Differences in working styles, temperaments, or attitudes.

3. **Resource Competition:** Disputes over limited resources such as budgets, time, or staffing.

4. **Unclear Expectations:** Ambiguities in roles, responsibilities, or goals.

5. **Diverging Goals:** Differing priorities between individuals or departments.

The Importance of Managing Conflict Effectively

1. **Fosters Collaboration**

   Constructive conflict resolution strengthens teamwork and builds trust.

2. **Encourages Innovation**

   Diverse perspectives can lead to creative problem-solving.

3. **Reduces Stress**

   Addressing conflicts early prevents escalation and fosters a healthier work environment.

4. **Enhances Professional Relationships**

   Successful conflict management improves understanding and respect among colleagues.

Why Manage Conflict Effectively?

1. Improve relationships and communication
2. Increase productivity and efficiency
3. Enhance problem-solving and decision-making
4. Reduce stress and anxiety
5. Foster a positive work culture
6. Build trust and credibility
7. Resolve issues promptly
8. Minimize conflicts escalating
9. Enhance collaboration and teamwork
10. Support personal and professional growth

Understanding Conflict

1. Types of conflict: interpersonal, intrapersonal, organizational
2. Conflict triggers: communication, cultural differences, personalities
3. Conflict stages: latent, manifest, resolution
4. Conflict resolution styles: avoiding, competing, collaborating, compromising
5. Conflict dynamics: power, emotions, interests

Effective Conflict Management Strategies

1. Active listening: Understand perspectives and needs

2. Empathy: Acknowledge emotions and concerns

3. Open communication: Clarify issues and expectations

4. Problem-solving: Collaborate on solutions

5. Stay calm and composed: Manage emotions

6. Seek common ground: Find mutually beneficial solutions

7. Focus on interests, not positions

8. Use non-confrontational language

9. Practice mindfulness and self-awareness

10. Leverage technology for conflict resolution

More strategies

1. **Stay Calm and Objective**

   - Avoid reacting emotionally. Take a moment to assess the situation calmly.

   - Focus on the issue, not the person, to avoid personal attacks.

2. **Practice Active Listening**

   - Give the other person your full attention and listen without interrupting.

   - Reflect what you've heard to ensure understanding: "What I'm hearing is that you're concerned about…"

3. **Seek Common Ground**

   - Identify shared goals or mutual interests to build a foundation for resolution.

   - Example: "We both want this project to succeed. Let's find a way to move forward."

4. **Focus on Solutions, Not Blame**

    - Instead of dwelling on past mistakes, direct the conversation toward finding actionable solutions.

    - Ask open-ended questions like: "What steps can we take to resolve this issue?"

5. **Be Assertive, Not Aggressive**

    - Clearly express your perspective and needs while respecting the other party's viewpoint.

    - Use "I" statements to communicate your feelings: "I feel concerned when deadlines are missed because it affects the team's progress."

6. **Involve a Neutral Party if Necessary**

    - If the conflict cannot be resolved directly, seek mediation from a manager or HR professional.

Navigating Difficult Conversations

Difficult conversations often involve delivering bad news, addressing poor performance, or discussing sensitive topics. These situations require preparation and emotional intelligence to ensure a constructive dialogue.

Steps to Handle Difficult Conversations

1. **Prepare in Advance**

    - Identify the purpose of the conversation and what you hope to achieve.

    - Gather relevant facts or examples to support your points.

    - Anticipate potential reactions and plan your responses.

2. **Choose the Right Setting**

    - Conduct the conversation in a private, neutral space where both parties feel comfortable.

- Ensure you have enough time to discuss the issue thoroughly without interruptions.

3. **Start with Empathy**

   - Acknowledge the other person's perspective and express understanding.

   - Example: "I know this might be a difficult topic to discuss, but I believe it's important for us to address it."

4. **Be Direct and Clear**

   - State the issue concisely and without ambiguity. Avoid sugarcoating or downplaying the matter.

   - Example: "I've noticed that deadlines are consistently being missed, which is impacting the team's progress."

5. **Encourage Open Dialogue**

   - Invite the other person to share their thoughts, concerns, or explanations.

   - Use open-ended questions to facilitate discussion: "Can you help me understand what challenges you're facing?"

6. **Collaborate on Solutions**

   - Work together to identify steps for improvement or resolution.

   - Example: "How can we adjust processes to ensure deadlines are met moving forward?"

7. **End on a Positive Note**

   - Summarize the discussion, reiterate any agreements, and express optimism for the future.

   - Example: "I appreciate your openness, and I'm confident we can work through this together."

Challenges and How to Overcome Them

1. Defensiveness

- Solution: Stay calm and acknowledge their feelings without escalating the situation.

2. Avoidance

- Solution: Emphasize the importance of addressing the issue for mutual benefit.

3. Emotional Reactions

- Solution: Allow the person to vent, then redirect the conversation back to the issue at hand.

4. Lack of Resolution

- Solution: Follow up after the conversation to ensure agreed-upon actions are being implemented.

Practical Examples of Conflict Management and Difficult Conversations

1. Resolving a Team Disagreement

During a team project, two members disagree on the approach. The manager facilitates a discussion where each member shares their perspective, and together, they agree on a compromise that leverages both ideas.

2. Addressing Performance Issues

A supervisor discusses repeated tardiness with an employee. By focusing on the impact of lateness and collaborating on solutions, such as flexible start times, they resolve the issue constructively.

3. Discussing Salary Expectations

During a salary negotiation, a candidate and employer disagree on the offer. Through open dialogue, the candidate secures a signing bonus and additional benefits, satisfying both parties.

Key Takeaways

- Conflict and difficult conversations are opportunities for growth and understanding.

- Active listening, empathy, and clear communication are essential skills for navigating these situations.

- Focus on solutions, not blame, and work collaboratively to achieve positive outcomes.

- With practice and preparation, you can turn challenging interactions into productive and meaningful discussions.

Difficult Conversations

1. Preparing for difficult conversations

2. Delivering difficult messages

3. Receiving difficult feedback

4. Managing emotions and reactions

5. Maintaining relationships

6. Creating a safe and supportive environment

7. Using "I" statements

8. Avoiding blame and defensiveness

Real-Life Examples

Meet Rachel, who managed conflict effectively:

"I listened actively and empathized with my colleague's concerns, resolving the issue promptly."

Or John, who navigated a difficult conversation:

"I prepared thoroughly and delivered the message clearly, maintaining our professional relationship."

Common Conflict Management Mistakes

1. Avoiding conflict
2. Lack of communication
3. Emotional reactivity
4. Taking sides
5. Failing to address underlying issues
6. Insufficient empathy
7. Inadequate problem-solving
8. Unprofessional behaviour
9. Lack of cultural sensitivity
10. Ineffective use of technology

Overcoming Conflict Management Challenges

1. Develop self-awareness: Recognize your conflict resolution style
2. Build emotional intelligence: Manage emotions effectively
3. Practice active listening: Understand perspectives
4. Seek support: Consult mentors or conflict resolution experts
5. Stay adaptable: Adjust your approach as needed
6. Focus on shared goals: Collaborate on solutions
7. Leverage technology: Utilize conflict resolution tools
8. Foster a positive work culture
9. Encourage open communication
10. Provide training and development opportunities

Action Plan

1. Identify potential conflict triggers
2. Develop effective conflict management strategies
3. Practice active listening and empathy

4. Prepare for difficult conversations

5. Seek support and feedback

6. Review and revise your conflict management approach

7. Leverage technology for conflict resolution

8. Foster a positive work culture

9. Encourage open communication

10. Provide training and development opportunities

Call to Action

Conflict doesn't have to be a roadblock—it can be a stepping stone to stronger relationships and better outcomes. Start applying these strategies today to build your confidence and mastery in managing conflict and handling difficult conversations. These skills will serve you well in every stage of your career and beyond!

Conclusion

Managing conflict and difficult conversations is crucial for maintaining a positive work environment. By understanding conflict, developing effective strategies, and avoiding common mistakes, you'll resolve issues promptly and build stronger relationships.

In the next chapter, we'll discuss leveraging technology for career advancement, essential for staying competitive in a rapidly changing job market.

Reflection Exercise

1. What are your conflict management strengths and weaknesses?

2. How do you handle difficult conversations?

3. What strategies will you employ to manage conflict effectively?

4. How will you maintain relationships during conflict?

5. What support systems do you have in place?

Additional Resources

- "Difficult Conversations" by Douglas Stone
- "Crucial Conversations" by Kerry Patterson
- "Conflict Resolution for Dummies" by Vivian Scott
- "The Conflict Resolution Network" online course
- "MindTools" conflict resolution resources
- "Harvard Business Review" conflict management articles

9

Leveraging Technology for Career Advancement - Essential Skills for Staying Competitive

In Chapter 8, we discussed managing conflict and difficult conversations, essential skills for maintaining a positive work environment. Now, we'll focus on leveraging technology for career advancement, crucial for staying competitive in a rapidly changing job market.

In today's fast-paced digital world, technology is a driving force behind career success and advancement. From streamlining workflows to opening new opportunities for learning and networking, staying ahead in your career means embracing and mastering the tools and trends shaping your industry. This chapter will explore how to harness technology effectively to remain competitive, boost productivity, and position yourself as a valuable asset in the modern workplace.

Why Leverage Technology?

1. Enhance productivity and efficiency
2. Improve communication and collaboration
3. Increase visibility and credibility
4. Access new job opportunities and markets
5. Develop in-demand skills
6. Stay up-to-date with industry trends
7. Automate routine tasks
8. Enhance data analysis and decision-making
9. Foster innovation and creativity
10. Future-proof your career
11. Improve work-life balance
12. Enhance customer engagement
13. Support remote work
14. Facilitate knowledge sharing
15. Drive business growth

Essential Technology Skills

1. Digital literacy: Basic computer skills
2. Software proficiency: Microsoft Office, Google Suite
3. Data analysis: Excel, Tableau

4. Communication tools: Email, Slack, Zoom

5. Social media marketing: LinkedIn, Twitter

6. Cloud computing: AWS, Azure

7. Cybersecurity: Data protection, online safety

8. Artificial intelligence: AI basics, machine learning

9. Blockchain: Cryptocurrency, supply chain management

10. Web development: HTML, CSS, JavaScript

11. Mobile app development: iOS, Android

12. Database management: MySQL, Oracle

13. Network administration: Cisco, CompTIA

14. Project management: Agile, Scrum

15. User experience design: UX, UI

Emerging Technologies to Watch

1. Artificial intelligence (AI)

2. Blockchain

3. Internet of Things (IoT)

4. Virtual and augmented reality (VR/AR)

5. 5G networks

6. Quantum computing

7. Natural language processing (NLP)

8. Robotics process automation (RPA)

9. Edge computing

10. Extended reality (XR)

11. Autonomous vehicles

12. Biotechnology

13. Nanotechnology

14. 3D printing

15. Smart cities

Key Technology Skills for Career Advancement

1. **Digital Literacy**

    - Basic proficiency in tools like Microsoft Office, Google Workspace, and email platforms is non-negotiable.

    - Familiarity with cloud storage solutions like Google Drive, OneDrive, or Dropbox ensures seamless file sharing and collaboration.

2. **Data Analysis and Interpretation**

    - Learn to work with tools like Excel, Tableau, or Power BI to analyze and visualize data.

    - Understanding data trends and metrics enhances decision-making and demonstrates your analytical capabilities.

3. **Project Management Tools**

    - Master software like Trello, Asana, or Monday.com to manage tasks, deadlines, and team coordination effectively.

    - Agile project management platforms such as Jira are increasingly sought after in technical roles.

4. **Communication and Collaboration Tools**

    - Platforms like Slack, Microsoft Teams, and Zoom are integral for modern workplace communication.

    - Learn to host and participate in virtual meetings, webinars, and team discussions professionally.

5. **Social Media and Personal Branding**

    - Utilize LinkedIn, Twitter, or industry-specific platforms to showcase expertise, network, and stay updated on trends.

- Build a professional online presence to attract opportunities and establish authority in your field.

6. **Cybersecurity Awareness**

   - Learn best practices for online security, such as recognizing phishing attempts and safeguarding sensitive information.

   - Use password managers and enable multi-factor authentication for added security.

7. **Coding and Automation Basics**

   - Understanding coding languages like Python, JavaScript, or SQL can be a valuable asset, even for non-tech roles.

   - Tools like Zapier or Power Automate can help streamline repetitive tasks through automation.

8. **AI and Machine Learning**

   - Familiarize yourself with AI tools like ChatGPT, Grammarly, or AI-powered CRM systems to boost productivity.

   - Learn the basics of AI-driven decision-making to leverage its potential in your industry.

Staying Updated on Emerging Trends

Technology evolves rapidly, and staying informed is essential to remain competitive.

1. **Follow Industry News**

   - Subscribe to tech blogs, podcasts, and news outlets like TechCrunch, Wired, or industry-specific publications.

2. **Participate in Online Communities**

   - Join forums, LinkedIn groups, or Slack communities to connect with professionals and exchange insights.

3. **Attend Webinars and Conferences**

   - Virtual and in-person events provide opportunities to learn about the latest tools and trends.

4. **Commit to Lifelong Learning**

   - Platforms like Coursera, Udemy, or LinkedIn Learning offer courses to keep your skills sharp.

How to Integrate Technology into Your Career Strategy

1. **Identify Relevant Tools for Your Role**

   - Research tools commonly used in your industry and learn how to use them effectively.

   - Example: A graphic designer should master software like Adobe Creative Suite, while a marketer should explore tools like HubSpot or Google Analytics.

2. **Seek Certifications**

   - Obtain certifications to validate your technical skills and make your resume stand out.

   - Examples include certifications for Google Analytics, Salesforce, or AWS.

3. **Experiment and Practice**

   - Dedicate time to exploring new tools and experimenting with how they can improve your workflow.

   - Example: If you're new to automation, try creating a simple workflow in Zapier to see how it reduces manual effort.

4. **Showcase Tech Proficiency on Your Resume**

   - Highlight tools and platforms you've mastered in the skills section of your resume or portfolio.

   - Include examples of how you've used technology to achieve tangible results.

Overcoming Challenges in Adopting Technology

1. **Fear of Change**

   - Solution: Start small by learning one tool at a time and gradually integrating it into your workflow.

2. **Time Constraints**

   - Solution: Dedicate a specific time each week for skill development or explore microlearning platforms.

3. **Steep Learning Curves**

   - Solution: Utilize tutorials, user guides, and online communities to accelerate your learning.

4. **Cost of Tools or Training**

   - Solution: Look for free or low-cost alternatives and explore free trials to test software before investing.

Success Stories: How Technology Transforms Careers

1. **The Freelancer**

   A graphic designer mastered Canva and Adobe Illustrator, leading to a surge in freelance opportunities through platforms like Upwork.

2. **The Analyst**

   A marketing professional learned Google Analytics and boosted their department's campaign ROI, earning a promotion.

3. **The Entrepreneur**

   A small business owner adopted e-commerce tools like Shopify and social media marketing, doubling their customer base within a year.

Key Takeaways

- Technology is an indispensable tool for career advancement and staying competitive.

- Develop skills in tools and platforms that align with your industry and role.

- Stay informed about emerging trends and invest in continuous learning to adapt to changes.

- Leverage technology to enhance productivity, expand your network, and achieve your career goals.

Real-Life Examples

Meet Emily, who leveraged technology to advance her career:

"I developed data analysis skills and created visualizations, impressing my boss and earning a promotion."

Or David, who used social media to build his brand:

"I established a strong LinkedIn presence and connected with industry leaders, landing speaking engagements."

Common Technology Mistakes

1. Lack of digital literacy
2. Insufficient software proficiency
3. Inadequate data analysis skills
4. Poor online presence
5. Ineffective communication tools
6. Ignoring cybersecurity threats
7. Failing to adapt to emerging technologies
8. Overreliance on automation
9. Inadequate training and development
10. Neglecting ethics in technology use
11. Inefficient data management
12. Inadequate backup systems
13. Insufficient disaster recovery planning

14. Lack of technology standards

15. Inadequate IT support

Overcoming Technology Challenges

1. Stay curious: Continuously learn and update skills

2. Seek support: Consult mentors or technology experts

3. Practice digital literacy: Develop basic computer skills

4. Focus on user experience: Design intuitive interfaces

5. Prioritize cybersecurity: Protect sensitive data

6. Leverage online resources: Utilize tutorials and webinars

7. Join online communities: Engage with technology professionals

8. Attend industry events: Stay updated on emerging trends

9. Collaborate with others: Share knowledge and expertise

10. Stay adaptable: Adjust to changing technology landscape

Action Plan

1. Assess your technology skills

2. Develop essential technology skills

3. Explore emerging technologies

4. Create a strong online presence

5. Leverage communication tools

6. Prioritize cybersecurity

7. Stay updated on industry trends

8. Seek support and training

9. Collaborate with others

10. Review and revise your technology strategy

Call to Action

The digital age waits for no one. Start leveraging technology today to unlock new career opportunities and maximize your potential. Identify one tool or skill you can learn this month, and take the first step toward becoming a tech-savvy professional!

Conclusion

Leveraging technology is crucial for staying competitive in today's job market. By developing essential technology skills, staying updated on emerging trends, and avoiding common mistakes, you'll enhance your career prospects and future-proof your profession.

In the next chapter, we'll discuss creating a work-life balance, essential for maintaining well-being and happiness.

Reflection Exercise

1. What are your technology strengths and weaknesses?
2. How do you leverage technology for career advancement?
3. What emerging technologies interest you?
4. How will you stay updated on industry trends?
5. What support systems do you have in place?

Additional Resources

1. "The Future of Work" by Darrell M. West
2. "Digital Literacy" by Paul Gilster

10

Creating a Work-Life Balance - Essential for Maintaining Well-being and Happiness

In Chapter 9, we discussed leveraging technology for career advancement, which is crucial for staying competitive in a rapidly changing job market. Now, we'll focus on creating a work-life balance, essential for maintaining well-being and happiness.

In the pursuit of career success, it's easy to neglect personal well-being and happiness. However, maintaining a healthy work-life balance is critical for long-term success, mental health, and overall satisfaction. This chapter explores strategies for achieving harmony between your professional and personal life, ensuring you can thrive in both areas without burnout or compromise.

Signs of an Imbalanced Work-Life Situation

- **Excessive Work Hours:** Working late nights or weekends consistently.

- **Neglected Personal Life:** Missing important family events or social gatherings.

- **Chronic Stress or Fatigue:** Feeling exhausted or overwhelmed daily.

- **Declining Health:** Experiencing frequent illnesses, headaches, or poor fitness.

- **Loss of Enjoyment:** Lack of interest in hobbies or activities you once loved.

Why Achieve Work-Life Balance?

1. Improve mental and physical health

2. Enhance relationships and social connections

3. Increase productivity and focus

4. Reduce stress and burnout

5. Improve work satisfaction and engagement

6. Support personal growth and development

7. Increase flexibility and adaptability

8. Enhance creativity and innovation

9. Support overall well-being

10. Improve work-life integration

11. Enhance job satisfaction

12. Reduce absenteeism

13. Improve employee retention

14. Support diversity and inclusion

15. Foster a positive work culture

Defining Work-Life Balance

1. Separation: Clear boundaries between work and personal life

2. Integration: Blending work and personal life

3. Flexibility: Adapting to changing work and personal demands

4. Autonomy: Control over work and personal life

5. Support: Resources and networks for balance

6. Boundaries: Establishing clear work and personal spaces

7. Priorities: Aligning work and personal goals

8. Self-care: Regular exercise and relaxation

9. Communication: Open dialogue with employer and family

10. Adaptability: Embracing change and uncertainty

Strategies for Achieving Work-Life Balance

1. Set clear boundaries: Establish work and personal spaces

2. Prioritize self-care: Exercise, meditation, and relaxation

3. Schedule downtime: Plan vacations and breaks

4. Communicate with your employer: Negotiate flexible work arrangements

5. Leverage technology: Utilize productivity tools and apps

6. Outsource and delegate: Share responsibilities

7. Practice mindfulness: Focus on the present

8. Seek support: Build a support network

9. Re-evaluate priorities: Align work and personal goals

10. Take breaks: Recharge and refresh

11. Learn to say no: Set realistic expectations

12. Seek professional help: Counselling or coaching

13. Foster a positive work culture

14. Support employee well-being

15. Encourage work-life balance

More strategies

1. **Set Clear Boundaries**

    - Define specific work hours and stick to them.

    - Avoid checking work emails or messages during personal time.

2. **Learn to Say No**

    - Politely decline additional tasks or commitments that overburden you.

    - Example: "I'd love to help, but I'm currently at capacity with my existing projects."

3. **Prioritize Tasks with Time Management Tools**

    - Use tools like Google Calendar, Trello, or Todoist to organize and prioritize your tasks.

    - Focus on high-impact activities and delegate less critical tasks.

4. **Schedule Personal Time**

    - Treat personal activities, such as exercise or family dinners, as non-negotiable appointments.

    - Plan vacations or staycations to disconnect from work and recharge.

5. **Adopt Flexible Work Options**

   - If possible, negotiate remote or hybrid work arrangements for better time management.

   - Use saved commuting time for hobbies, fitness, or family.

6. **Communicate Your Needs**

   - Discuss work-life balance goals with your employer, colleagues, or family.

   - Example: "I'd like to adjust my schedule slightly to ensure I can meet both work and personal commitments."

7. **Focus on Quality, Not Quantity**

   - Be fully present in your current activity, whether it's work or personal time.

   - Example: During family time, put away devices and actively engage with loved ones.

Self-Care: The Foundation of Balance

1. **Physical Wellness**

   - Regular exercise, a balanced diet, and sufficient sleep are essential for maintaining energy and focus.

2. **Mental and Emotional Health**

   - Practice mindfulness or meditation to reduce stress.

   - Seek support from a therapist or counsellor if needed.

3. **Hobbies and Interests**

   - Pursue activities that bring you joy and relaxation, such as painting, gardening, or playing a musical instrument.

4. **Digital Detox**

   - Unplug from screens periodically to reconnect with yourself and your surroundings.

Work-Life Balance in Different Career Stages

1. **Early Career**

   - Focus on building skills and gaining experience without sacrificing personal time.

   - Learn to manage workload and avoid the trap of constant availability.

2. **Mid-Career**

   - Balance growing professional responsibilities with family or personal commitments.

   - Delegate tasks and prioritize leadership over micromanagement.

3. **Late Career**

   - Shift focus toward mentoring, legacy building, and personal fulfilment.

   - Use accumulated experience to work smarter, not harder.

Challenges to Work-Life Balance and How to Overcome Them

1. **Unrealistic Expectations**

   - Solution: Set achievable goals and break tasks into manageable steps.

2. **Workplace Culture**

   - Solution: Advocate for work-life balance initiatives or seek employers that prioritize employee well-being.

3. **Guilt or Fear of Missing Out (FOMO)**

   - Solution: Recognize that taking breaks enhances performance and does not diminish commitment.

4. **Financial Pressures**

   - Solution: Budget wisely and explore side hustles or passive income opportunities that don't overextend you.

Practical Examples of Work-Life Balance

1. **The Entrepreneur**

   A small business owner dedicates weekends to family and automates customer inquiries using chatbots, freeing up personal time.

2. **The Remote Worker**

   A remote employee schedules daily outdoor walks and uses a productivity timer to separate work hours from personal time.

3. **The Executive**

   A senior manager blocks off time for gym workouts and family dinners, demonstrating that balance is achievable even in demanding roles.

Real-Life Examples

Meet Sarah, who achieved work-life balance:

"I prioritized self-care, scheduled downtime, and communicated with my employer, resulting in increased productivity and happiness."

Or John, who leveraged technology:

"I used productivity tools and apps to manage my workload, allowing for more personal time."

Key Takeaways

- Work-life balance is essential for maintaining mental, physical, and emotional well-being.

- Set boundaries, prioritize tasks, and practice self-care to achieve harmony between work and personal life.

- Tailor your approach to balance based on your career stage and unique circumstances.

- Remember that a fulfilling life includes time for relationships, hobbies, and rest.

Common Work-Life Balance Mistakes

1. Overworking
2. Lack of boundaries
3. Inadequate self-care
4. Poor communication
5. Unrealistic expectations
6. Inadequate support
7. Failure to prioritize
8. Inability to disconnect
9. Lack of flexibility
10. Neglecting personal goals
11. Insufficient resources
12. Lack of autonomy
13. Inadequate work-life policies
14. Unsupportive work culture
15. Inadequate technology

Overcoming Work-Life Balance Challenges

1. Identify priorities: Align work and personal goals
2. Seek support: Build a support network
3. Practice self-care: Regular exercise and relaxation
4. Set boundaries: Establish clear work and personal spaces
5. Leverage technology: Productivity tools and apps
6. Communicate effectively: Negotiate flexible work arrangements
7. Stay flexible: Adapt to changing demands
8. Prioritize downtime: Schedule vacations and breaks
9. Re-evaluate priorities: Align work and personal goals

10. Seek professional help: Counselling or coaching

11. Foster a positive work culture

12. Support employee well-being

13. Encourage work-life balance

14. Provide resources and support

15. Review and revise policies

Action Plan

1. Assess your work-life balance

2. Set clear boundaries

3. Prioritize self-care

4. Schedule downtime

5. Communicate with your employer

6. Leverage technology

7. Outsource and delegate

8. Practice mindfulness

9. Seek support

10. Review and revise your balance strategy

11. Foster a positive work culture

12. Support employee well-being

13. Encourage work-life balance

14. Provide resources and support

15. Review and revise policies

Call to Action

Achieving work-life balance is not just a luxury—it's a necessity for a happy and productive life. Start today by identifying one area where you can create more balance, whether it's setting boundaries, pursuing a hobby, or spending quality time with loved ones. Your well-being is the foundation of your success!

Conclusion

Creating a work-life balance is essential for maintaining well-being and happiness. By understanding the importance of balance, defining your balance, and implementing effective strategies, you'll achieve a harmonious integration of work and personal life.

In the next chapter, we'll discuss building resilience and adapting to change, crucial for navigating today's fast-paced work environment.

Part 3

Navigating Career Transitions

11

Building Resilience and Adapting to Change - Navigating Today's Fast-Paced Work Environment

"Resilience is the ability to attack while running away."

– Hiroo Onoda

In Chapter 10, we discussed creating a work-life balance, essential for maintaining well-being and happiness. Now, we'll focus on building resilience and adapting to change, crucial for navigating today's fast-paced work environment.

In today's dynamic and ever-evolving workplace, the ability to build resilience and adapt to change is no longer optional—it's essential. Rapid technological advancements, economic shifts, and unexpected global events can disrupt the status quo at any moment. This chapter explores strategies for cultivating resilience and flexibility to thrive in a fast-paced professional landscape.

Understanding Resilience and Adaptability

1. **Resilience**

   - The capacity to recover quickly from challenges, setbacks, or stress.

   - Involves maintaining a positive outlook and finding solutions even in difficult situations.

2. **Adaptability**

   - The ability to adjust to new circumstances, roles, or environments.

   - Emphasizes learning, flexibility, and a willingness to embrace change.

The Importance of Resilience and Adaptability in the Workplace

1. **Coping with Uncertainty**

   - Resilient employees handle disruptions, such as layoffs or technological changes, with composure and creativity.

2. **Seizing Opportunities**

   - Adaptable individuals are more likely to identify and capitalize on new trends, tools, and career paths.

3. **Improved Problem-Solving**

   - A resilient mindset fosters innovative thinking and persistence in addressing challenges.

4. **Career Longevity**

   - Professionals who adapt to industry shifts and develop resilience stay relevant and valuable over time.

Characteristics of Resilient Professionals

- **Optimism:** Focus on solutions and positive outcomes rather than dwelling on problems.

- **Emotional Intelligence:** Manage emotions effectively and understand others' perspectives.

- **Resourcefulness:** Use available resources creatively to overcome obstacles.

- **Self-Efficacy:** Believe in your ability to navigate challenges and achieve goals.

- **Persistence:** Maintain effort and focus despite setbacks or slow progress.

Strategies for Building Resilience

1. **Develop a Growth Mindset**

   - Embrace challenges as opportunities to learn and grow.

   - Replace self-defeating thoughts with empowering affirmations.

   - Example: Instead of "I can't handle this," think, "I'll figure out a way."

2. **Strengthen Emotional Agility**

   - Acknowledge and process your emotions without letting them control you.

   - Practice mindfulness or meditation to stay grounded during stressful moments.

3. **Cultivate Strong Relationships**

   - Build a support network of colleagues, mentors, and friends.

   - Seek feedback and advice to gain perspective and encouragement.

4. **Prioritize Self-Care**

   - Maintain a balanced lifestyle with regular exercise, healthy eating, and adequate sleep.

   - Engage in hobbies or activities that recharge your energy and boost your mood.

Learn from Failure

- Analyze setbacks to identify lessons and areas for improvement.

- Use failures as stepping stones to future success.

Techniques to Adapt to Change

1. **Stay Informed**

   - Keep up with industry trends, technological advancements, and market dynamics.

   - Attend webinars, read blogs, and join professional communities to stay updated.

2. **Be Open to Learning**

   - Continuously update your skills through courses, certifications, or workshops.

   - Learn new technologies or tools relevant to your field.

3. **Embrace Flexibility**

   - Be willing to take on new roles, responsibilities, or projects.

   - View change as an opportunity to expand your expertise and network.

4. **Develop Problem-Solving Skills**

   - Approach challenges with a solution-focused mindset.

   - Break problems into smaller, manageable steps and tackle them systematically.

5. **Seek Feedback and Adapt**

   - Regularly solicit input from peers, managers, or clients.

   - Use feedback constructively to refine your approach and performance.

Overcoming Resistance to Change

1. **Acknowledge Fears**

   - Identify and address the underlying reasons for your discomfort with change.

   - Example: Fear of failure can be mitigated by developing a solid plan and seeking support.

2. **Focus on the Positive**

   - Look for potential benefits and opportunities in new situations.

   - Example: A company restructuring might offer a chance for leadership growth.

3. **Take Incremental Steps**

   - Break larger changes into smaller, more manageable adjustments.

   - Gradual adaptation reduces overwhelm and builds confidence.

Real-World Examples of Resilience and Adaptability

1. **The Freelancer**

   - A freelance writer pivoted from traditional publishing to digital content creation by mastering SEO and social media marketing.

2. **The Corporate Employee**

   - A project manager adapted to remote work during the pandemic by learning virtual collaboration tools like Microsoft Teams and Zira.

3. **The Entrepreneur**

   - A business owner shifted from brick-and-mortar sales to e-commerce, leveraging platforms like Shopify and digital advertising to stay competitive

Building Organizational Resilience

1. **Foster a Culture of Innovation**

   - Encourage employees to experiment with new ideas and approaches.

   - Celebrate creativity and learn from mistakes.

2. **Invest in Training and Development**

   - Provide resources and opportunities for employees to upskill and adapt.

3. **Promote Open Communication**

   - Keep teams informed about changes and involve them in decision-making processes.

4. **Develop Contingency Plans**

   - Anticipate potential disruptions and have strategies in place to address them.

Why Build Resilience?

1. Manage stress and anxiety
2. Cope with uncertainty and change
3. Develop adaptability and flexibility
4. Enhance problem-solving and decision-making
5. Improve relationships and communication
6. Increase productivity and performance
7. Support personal growth and development
8. Foster a positive work culture
9. Enhance creativity and innovation
10. Drive business success

Understanding Resilience

1. Emotional intelligence: Self-awareness and regulation
2. Optimism: Positive attitude and outlook
3. Self-confidence: Faith in abilities and judgment
4. Adaptability: Flexibility and adjustability
5. Problem-solving: Resourcefulness and creativity
6. Social support: Network and community
7. Meaning-making: Purpose and significance
8. Self-care: Physical and mental well-being
9. Learning agility: Ability to learn and adapt
10. Emotional regulation: Managing emotions

Strategies for Building Resilience

1. Practice self-awareness: Recognize emotions and thoughts
2. Develop emotional regulation: Manage emotions effectively
3. Cultivate optimism: Focus on positive outcomes
4. Build self-confidence: Develop skills and abilities
5. Foster adaptability: Embrace change and uncertainty
6. Develop problem-solving skills: Think critically and creatively
7. Nurture social support: Build a support network
8. Find meaning and purpose: Align work and personal values
9. Prioritize self-care: Maintain physical and mental well-being
10. Develop learning agility: Stay curious and open-minded

Real-Life Examples

Meet Emily, who built resilience

"I practiced self-awareness, developed emotional regulation, and cultivated optimism, resulting in increased confidence and adaptability."

Or David, who adapted to change

"I fostered adaptability, developed problem-solving skills, and nurtured social support, leading to successful navigation of organizational change."

Common Resilience Mistakes

1. Lack of self-awareness
2. Inadequate emotional regulation
3. Negative thinking patterns
4. Insufficient self-confidence
5. Inflexibility
6. Poor problem-solving skills
7. Inadequate social support
8. Lack of purpose and meaning
9. Neglecting self-care
10. Resistance to change
11. Inadequate communication
12. Lack of accountability
13. Insufficient resources
14. Unsupportive work culture
15. Inadequate training and development

Overcoming Resilience Challenges

1. Identify areas for improvement: Assess resilience strengths and weaknesses
2. Seek support: Build a support network
3. Practice self-care: Regular exercise and relaxation
4. Develop emotional regulation: Manage emotions effectively
5. Cultivate optimism: Focus on positive outcomes

6. Foster adaptability: Embrace change and uncertainty
7. Develop problem-solving skills: Think critically and creatively
8. Nurture social support: Build relationships
9. Find meaning and purpose: Align work and personal values
10. Develop learning agility: Stay curious and open-minded

Action Plan

1. Assess your resilience
2. Practice self-awareness
3. Develop emotional regulation
4. Cultivate optimism
5. Build self-confidence
6. Foster adaptability
7. Develop problem-solving skills
8. Nurture social support
9. Find meaning and purpose
10. Prioritize self-care
11. Develop learning agility
12. Review and revise your resilience strategy

Key Takeaways

- Resilience and adaptability are critical for navigating today's fast-paced work environment.
- Developing these skills enhances problem-solving, reduces stress, and ensures career longevity.
- Embrace a growth mindset, prioritize learning, and seek support from your network.
- Change is inevitable—view it as an opportunity for growth and success.

Call to Action

Adapting and thriving in the face of change is your superpower in today's dynamic world. Start building your resilience today by identifying one area of your life or career where you can embrace change. Take a small, actionable step and watch how it opens doors to new opportunities and growth

Conclusion

Building resilience and adapting to change are essential for navigating today's fast-paced work environment. Understanding the importance of resilience, developing effective strategies, and avoiding common mistakes will enhance your ability to cope with uncertainty and drive business success.

12

Uncertainty Upside:
Embracing Change and Risk

In a world marked by constant change, uncertainty often feels intimidating. However, it also presents a hidden opportunity—an upside that can lead to growth, innovation, and success. Embracing change and taking calculated risks are essential skills for thriving in both your personal and professional life. This chapter explores how to shift your mindset toward uncertainty, harness its potential, and turn risks into stepping stones for success.

The Nature of Uncertainty and Risk

1. **What is Uncertainty?**

   - The unpredictable nature of situations, outcomes, or events.

   - Common in rapidly evolving industries, economic shifts, or major life transitions.

2. **What is Risk?**

   - The potential for loss or failure when pursuing an opportunity or making a decision.

   - Often necessary to achieve significant progress or innovation.

3. **The Connection**

   - Risk and uncertainty go hand in hand, but with preparation and a positive outlook, they can be powerful catalysts for success.

Why Embrace Uncertainty and Risk?

1. **Growth and Learning**

   - Stepping outside your comfort zone fosters personal and professional development.

2. **New Opportunities**

   - Uncertainty often brings unexpected chances to innovate or pursue new paths.

3. **Competitive Advantage**

   - Those willing to take risks often stand out as leaders and innovators in their field.

4. **Resilience Building**

   - Navigating uncertainty strengthens your ability to handle future challenges.

Changing Your Mindset Toward Uncertainty

1. **From Fear to Curiosity**

   - Instead of fearing the unknown, view it as an adventure filled with possibilities.

   - Ask yourself: "What can I learn from this?"

2. **Focus on What You Can Control**

   - Identify areas where you can take action and influence outcomes.

- Example: You can't control market trends, but you can upskill or network to stay competitive.

3. **Reframe Failure as Feedback**

   - Shift your perspective: failures are valuable lessons, not endpoints.

   - Example: If a business idea fails, analyze what went wrong and apply those insights to future endeavours.

4. **Cultivate Optimism**

   - Visualize positive outcomes and remind yourself of past successes.

   - Optimism helps reduce stress and enhances decision-making.

Strategies for Embracing Change and Risk

1. **Start Small**

   - Take manageable risks to build confidence.

   - Example: Volunteer for a new project at work before launching your initiative.

2. **Develop a Plan**

   - Break larger risks into smaller, actionable steps.

   - Example: If considering a career change, start by researching industries and building relevant skills.

3. **Seek Support**

   - Surround yourself with mentors, colleagues, or friends who encourage calculated risks.

   - Learn from others' experiences to navigate uncertainty more effectively.

4. **Invest in Continuous Learning**

   - Equip yourself with knowledge and skills to adapt to unexpected changes.

- Explore workshops, courses, or industry certifications to stay ahead.

5. **Practice Resilience**

   - Build emotional and mental resilience to handle setbacks gracefully.

   - Techniques like mindfulness and stress management are invaluable in uncertain times.

Uncertainty is an inevitable part of career transitions. Instead of fearing it, learn to harness its power for growth and transformation. This chapter explores strategies for embracing uncertainty, building risk tolerance, and seizing unexpected opportunities.

Examples of Embracing Change and Risk

1. **The Entrepreneur**

   - Leaped to start a business despite economic uncertainty and found success by adapting to market needs.

2. **The Career Changer**

   - Left a stable corporate job to pursue a passion for teaching and found fulfilment in shaping future generations.

3. **The Innovator**

   - Proposed a risky, unconventional solution to a workplace challenge, which ultimately boosted team efficiency.

Section 1: Reframing Uncertainty

Uncertainty can evoke fear, anxiety, or paralysis. However, it also presents opportunities for growth, innovation, and transformation.

1. **Recognizing uncertainty as an opportunity:** View uncertainty as a chance to explore new paths, challenge assumptions, and develop resilience.

2. **Letting go of the need for control**: Acknowledge that uncertainty is inherent in life and career transitions. Focus on what you can control.

3. **Embracing the unknown**: Cultivate curiosity and openness to new experiences and outcomes.

Section 2: Building Risk Tolerance

Risk tolerance is essential for navigating uncertainty.

1. **Assessing risk vs. reward**: Evaluate potential risks and benefits of different choices.

2. **Developing resilience**: Build coping skills, support networks, and adaptability.

3. **Creating a safety net**: Establish financial stability, skill diversification, and contingency plans.

Section 3: Navigating Ambiguity

Ambiguity requires clarity on your core values and goals.

1. **Clarifying values and goals**: Define your non-negotiables and priorities.

2. **Exploring diverse perspectives**: Seek advice from mentors, peers, and industry experts.

3. **Staying adaptable**: Remain open to adjusting plans as circumstances change.

Section 4: Seizing Unexpected Opportunities

Uncertainty can bring unexpected opportunities.

1. **Spotting hidden chances**: Stay alert to emerging trends, networking opportunities, and innovative solutions.

2. **Taking calculated leaps**: Balance risk assessment with bold action.

3. **Leveraging uncertainty for innovation***:* Encourage experimentation, creativity, and learning.

Section 5: Mindset Shifts for Embracing Uncertainty

Embracing uncertainty requires fundamental mindset shifts.

1. **From fear to curiosity***:* View uncertainty as an exciting adventure.

2. **From predictability to flexibility***:* Prioritize adaptability over rigid plans.

3. **From comfort to growth***:* Recognize that growth often requires discomfort.

Section 6: *Real-Life Examples of Embracing Uncertainty*

Meet individuals who successfully navigated uncertainty.

1. **Entrepreneurial success stories***:* Learn from founders who turned uncertainty into opportunity.

2. **Career pivoters***:* Hear from professionals who leveraged uncertainty for transformation.

3. **Innovation leaders***:* Discover how companies embrace uncertainty for innovation.

Section 7: *Actionable Strategies for Thriving in Uncertainty*

Apply these actionable strategies.

1. **Uncertainty mapping***:* Visualize potential outcomes and prepare accordingly.

2. **Risk-reward analysis***:* Evaluate choices with a clear framework.

3. **Resilience building***:* Develop coping skills and support networks.

4. **Opportunity scouting***:* Stay alert to emerging trends and opportunities.

5. **Mindfulness and self-reflection***:* Regularly assess values, goals, and progress.

Balancing Risk and Preparation

1. **Conduct a Risk Assessment**

   - List potential risks, their likelihood, and their impact.

   - Identify ways to mitigate them, such as financial planning or skill development.

2. **Build a Safety Net**

   - Save funds or resources to cushion potential setbacks.

   - Example: Maintain an emergency fund before launching a freelance career.

3. **Gather Data and Insights**

   - Make informed decisions by researching trends, consulting experts, and analyzing options.

   - Example: Before investing in stocks, study market performance and diversify your portfolio.

4. **Accept Imperfection**

   - Understand that no decision or outcome is guaranteed to be flawless.

   - Focus on progress over perfection.

The Role of Intuition in Decision-Making

1. **Trust Your Gut**

   - Combine logical analysis with intuitive insights for balanced decision-making.

   - Example: If a job offers feels aligned with your goals, trust that instinct even if it involves some risk.

2. **Fine-Tune Intuition**

   - **Reflect on past decisions and outcomes to sharpen your intuitive abilities.**

Realizing the Upside of Uncertainty

1. **Creative Breakthroughs**

   - *Uncertainty often forces you to think outside the box, leading to innovation.*

   - *Example: Companies like **Airbnb** and **Uber** emerged during economic downturns.*

2. **Personal Growth**

   - Navigating challenges boosts confidence, adaptability, and self-awareness.

3. **Career Advancement**

   - Taking calculated risks, like accepting leadership roles, can fast-track your professional growth.

4. **Building a Legacy**

   - Bold decisions often leave a lasting impact, inspiring others to embrace change.

Key Takeaways

- Uncertainty and risk are inherent in growth and success.

- By shifting your mindset and preparing strategically, you can turn challenges into opportunities.

- Small, calculated risks pave the way for greater confidence and resilience.

- Embrace change as a pathway to innovation, self-discovery, and long-term fulfilment.

Call to Action

Don't let fear of the unknown hold you back. Identify one area in your life or career where you can take a small, calculated risk today. Whether it's learning a new skill, pitching an idea, or exploring a new path, step into the uncertainty—and discover the upside waiting for you

Conclusion

Uncertainty can be a catalyst for career growth and transformation. By embracing change and risk, you'll unlock new possibilities and thrive in an uncertain world.

Actionable Exercises and Reflections

1. Identify areas where uncertainty holds you back.

2. Develop a risk tolerance framework.

3. Explore diverse perspectives.

4. Reflect on past experiences where uncertainty led to growth.

5. Create an uncertainty map for your current career transition.

Embracing uncertainty requires intentional effort but yields immense rewards. By applying these strategies, you'll transform uncertainty into a powerful tool for career growth and success.

13

Overcoming Obstacles: Strategies for Career Transition Success

In Chapter 12, you learned to embrace uncertainty and risk. Now, it's time to tackle obstacles that may hinder your career transition progress.

Changing careers is a bold and transformative decision, often accompanied by challenges and uncertainties. While career transitions may seem daunting, with the right strategies, you can navigate obstacles effectively and achieve success in your new path. This chapter explores practical techniques to overcome common barriers during career transitions and offers guidance on making the journey as smooth and rewarding as possible.

Why Career Transitions Are Challenging

1. **Fear of the Unknown**

    - Leaving behind familiarity for uncharted territory can feel intimidating.

2. **Skill Gaps**

    - The requirements of a new career may demand skills you don't yet possess.

3. **Financial Concerns**

    - A career change often involves a temporary decrease in income or stability.

4. **Identity Shifts**

    - Letting go of a professional identity tied to your previous career can be emotionally taxing.

5. **External Pressures**

    - Family, friends, or colleagues may question or discourage your decision.

Preparing for a Successful Career Transition

1. **Clarify Your Goals**

    - Identify why you want to make the transition and what you hope to achieve.

    - Write down specific, measurable goals to keep you focused.

2. **Research Your Target Industry or Role**

    - Understand the requirements, expectations, and opportunities in your desired field.

    - Example: Explore job descriptions, connect with professionals in the industry, and follow relevant trends.

3. **Assess Your Transferable Skills**

   - List skills from your current role that are valuable in your new career.

   - Examples include communication, project management, problem-solving, and leadership.

4. **Build a Financial Plan**

   - Save money in advance to cover expenses during the transition.

   - Explore side hustles or part-time work to supplement your income while transitioning.

Strategies to Overcome Common Obstacles

1. **Skill Gaps**

   - ***Solution:*** *Upskill through online courses, workshops, or certifications.*

   - *Example: Platforms like Coursera, LinkedIn Learning, or Udemy offer industry-relevant training.*

2. **Lack of Experience**

   - ***Solution:*** *Gain experience through internships, freelance work, or volunteering.*

   - *Example: If transitioning to digital marketing, offer to manage social media for a non-profit to build your portfolio.*

3. **Networking Challenges**

   - ***Solution:*** *Actively engage with professionals in your target industry.*

   - *Attend events, join LinkedIn groups, and reach out for informational interviews.*

4. **Low Confidence**

   - ***Solution:*** *Celebrate small wins and remind yourself of past successes.*

- *Use affirmations or a journal to track progress and maintain motivation.*

Employer Resistance

- ***Solution:*** *Tailor your resume and cover letter to highlight relevant skills and enthusiasm.*

- *Practice your career change story for interviews, focusing on your transferable skills and passion.*

Navigating Emotional Challenges

1. **Managing Fear and Doubt**

   - Recognize that fear is a natural part of change and channel it into preparation.

   - Seek support from mentors, coaches, or peers who've successfully transitioned.

2. **Overcoming Imposter Syndrome**

   - Remind yourself that everyone starts somewhere and that your perspective brings value.

   - Example: Focus on your unique experiences and how they enrich your new role.

3. **Handling External Criticism**

   - Politely but firmly communicate your reasons for the change.

   - Example: "This transition aligns with my personal values and long-term goals."

4. **Staying Resilient During Setbacks**

   - Treat rejections or failures as learning experiences.

   - Adjust your strategy based on feedback and keep moving forward

Creating a Transition Plan

1. **Set a Timeline**

   - Break the transition into phases: exploration, skill-building, networking, and job searching.

   - Example: Dedicate the first three months to learning and networking, followed by active job applications.

2. **Leverage Your Network**

   - Reach out to former colleagues, alumni groups, or industry associations for guidance and opportunities.

3. **Test the Waters**

   - Explore your new career path through part-time work, side projects, or shadowing professionals.

4. **Stay Organized**

   - Use tools like Trello, Notion, or Excel to track applications, connections, and tasks.

Real-Life Examples of Career Transition Success

1. The Teacher-Turned-Data Analyst

   - A former educator transitioned to data analysis by completing a coding bootcamp and showcasing problem-solving skills.

2. The Corporate Employee-Turned-Entrepreneur

   - A finance professional launched a successful bakery after identifying a passion for baking and taking business courses.

3. The Engineer-Turned-Writer

   - An engineer transitioned to content writing by building a portfolio through freelancing and networking with editors.

Embracing the Positive Aspects of Career Transition

1. **Personal Growth**

   - A career change often leads to enhanced self-awareness and new perspectives.

2. **Increased Fulfilment**

   - Pursuing a role aligned with your passion can boost job satisfaction and happiness.

3. **Expanded Network**

   - Transitioning allows you to connect with diverse professionals and communities.

4. **Broader Skillset**

   - A new career equips you with skills and experiences that enrich your professional journey.

Section 1: Identifying Common Obstacles

Recognize these common challenges:

1. Self-doubt and imposter syndrome
2. Lack of networking and connections
3. Skill gaps and outdated expertise
4. Financial constraints and limited resources
5. Fear of failure and perfectionism
6. Time management and prioritization
7. Balancing personal and professional responsibilities
8. Ageism and generational biases
9. Geographic constraints and relocation
10. Health and wellness challenges

Section 2: Building Resilience and Perseverance

Develop strategies to overcome obstacles:

1. Reframe negative self-talk and cultivate confidence
2. Leverage social media and online platforms for networking
3. Invest in continuous learning and skill development
4. Create a financial safety net and explore alternative income streams
5. Embrace failure as a learning opportunity
6. Prioritize tasks and manage time effectively
7. Set boundaries and maintain work-life balance
8. Develop coping skills for stress and anxiety
9. Foster a growth mindset
10. Celebrate small wins

Section 3: Leveraging Support Systems

1. Surround yourself with people who support your transition:
2. Mentorship: Find guidance from experienced professionals
3. Peer support: Join communities and networking groups
4. Coaching: Invest in personalized guidance
5. Family and friends: Communicate your goals and needs
6. Online forums and social media groups
7. Professional associations and networking events
8. Career counselling services

Section 4: Strategic Problem-Solving

Develop a systematic approach to overcoming obstacles:

1. Identify and define the problem

2. Analyze causes and consequences

3. Generate solutions and evaluate feasibility

4. Implement and monitor progress

5. Adjust and adapt as needed

6. Seek feedback and guidance

7. Reflect on lessons learned

Section 5: Real-Life Examples of Overcoming Obstacles

Inspiring stories of career transition success:

1. From stay-at-home parent to entrepreneur

2. Overcoming ageism in the job market

3. Transitioning from military to civilian career

4. From burnout to balanced career

5. Career pivot after a layoff

Section 6: Actionable Strategies for Overcoming Obstacles

Apply these tactics:

1. Obstacle mapping: Visualize challenges and solutions

2. Progress tracking: Celebrate small wins

3. Resilience journaling: Reflect on setbacks and growth

4. Support network development: Schedule regular check-ins

5. Skill development planning: Invest in courses and training

6. Time management optimization

7. Financial planning and budgeting

Section 7: Maintaining Momentum and Motivation

Stay focused and driven:

1. Set realistic goals and milestones
2. Create accountability partnerships
3. Celebrate successes and learn from failures
4. Prioritize self-care and well-being
5. Stay adaptable and open to new opportunities
6. Continuously evaluate and adjust plans

Section 8: Overcoming Obstacles in Specific Career Transition Scenarios

Address unique challenges in:

1. Industry transition
2. Geographic relocation
3. Career change after retirement
4. Transitioning from entrepreneurship to employment
5. Career advancement in a current organization

Key Takeaways

- Career transitions are challenging but achievable with careful planning and a proactive mindset.

- Identify your transferable skills, upskill strategically, and build a support network to overcome obstacles.

- Embrace setbacks as opportunities for growth and remain focused on your long-term goals.

- Success in a new career begins with self-belief and a commitment to continuous learning.

Call to Action

Your career transition journey begins with a single step. Start by researching your desired field and identifying one skill to develop. With determination, resilience, and the right strategies, you can overcome any obstacle and achieve your career goals. The future is yours—seize it!

Conclusion

Career transition success requires perseverance and resilience. By identifying obstacles, leveraging support systems, and developing strategic problem-solving skills, you'll overcome challenges and achieve your goals.

Actionable Exercises and Reflections

1. Identify your top three obstacles and create an action plan.

2. Reflect on past experiences where resilience helped you overcome challenges.

3. Develop a support network and schedule regular check-ins.

4. Create a progress tracking system to celebrate small wins.

5. Invest in skill development and continuous learning.

By applying these strategies, you'll navigate obstacles with confidence and achieve a successful career transition.

14

Transferable Treasures: Leveraging Your Existing Skills for a Successful Career Transition

In Chapter 13, you learned to overcome obstacles in your career transition. Now, discover how to unlock the value of your existing skills, experience, and achievements to propel your transition forward.

Career transitions can feel like starting from scratch, but the truth is, you carry a wealth of transferable skills that can give you a head start in your new path. These "transferable treasures" are the abilities and experiences you've honed in your current and past roles, which remain valuable across various industries and roles. This chapter delves into identifying, refining, and presenting your transferable skills to achieve a smooth and successful career transition.

What Are Transferable Skills?

Transferable skills are abilities and attributes that are relevant across multiple jobs and industries. These skills are often categorized into two types:

1. **Hard Skills:** Specific, teachable abilities such as data analysis, graphic design, or coding.

2. **Soft Skills:** Interpersonal and adaptable qualities like communication, leadership, problem-solving, and teamwork.

The Value of Transferable Skills in Career Transitions

1. **Bridges the Experience Gap**

   They help you demonstrate your capability even if you lack direct experience in a new field.

2. **Highlights Your Versatility**

   - Employers value candidates who can adapt and bring diverse skills to the table.

3. **Speeds Up Learning**

   - Your existing skills often reduce the learning curve in your new career.

Identifying Your Transferable Skills

1. **Reflect on Your Experience**

   - Consider your roles, projects, and responsibilities.

- Ask yourself
- What tasks did I excel at?
- Which skills did I use to overcome challenges?
- What do others frequently rely on me for?

2. **Analyze Job Descriptions**
   - Research your target industry or role and list the skills required.
   - Compare them to your current skill set to find overlaps.

3. **Seek Feedback**
   - Ask colleagues, mentors, or supervisors about your strengths.
   - They might identify valuable skills you've overlooked.

4. **Categorize Your Skills**
   - Group your skills into broad categories like communication, problem-solving, leadership, technical expertise, etc.

Examples of Transferable Skills

1. **Communication**
   - Writing clear reports or emails.
   - Delivering presentations and public speaking.

2. **Problem-Solving**
   - Identifying inefficiencies and creating solutions.
   - Analyzing data to inform decisions.

3. **Time Management**
   - Prioritizing tasks to meet deadlines.
   - Managing multiple projects simultaneously.

4. **Teamwork and Collaboration**
   - Working effectively in diverse teams.
   - Resolving conflicts constructively.

5. **Leadership**

   - Leading teams or projects to successful outcomes.

   - Mentoring or training junior colleagues.

6. **Adaptability**

   - Quickly learning new tools or systems.

   - Thriving in fast-paced, changing environments.

7. **Technical Skills**

   - Proficiency in software, tools, or systems relevant to your field.

   - Example: A marketing professional's expertise in data analytics can apply to other roles involving metrics and insights.

Repackaging Your Skills for a New Industry

1. **Translate Jargon**

   - Avoid industry-specific terms when describing your skills to make them relatable.

   - Example: Replace "sales funnel optimization" with "customer journey analysis."

2. **Focus on Results**

   - Highlight measurable outcomes you've achieved using your skills.

   - Example: "Streamlined workflows, reducing project completion time by 15%."

3. **Tailor Your Resume and Cover Letter**

   - Customize your application materials to emphasize skills aligned with the new role.

4. **Develop a Career Transition Narrative**

   - Be ready to explain how your existing skills make you a strong candidate.

- Example: "My experience managing cross-functional teams has equipped me to excel in project management roles."

Strengthening Your Transferable Skills

1. **Refine Core Skills**

   - Identify areas for improvement and take action.

   - Example: If communication is critical in your target role, join a public speaking group like Toastmasters.

2. **Add New Dimensions**

   - Complement your skills with targeted training or certifications.

   - Example: A graphic designer transitioning to user experience (UX) design might complete a UX bootcamp.

3. **Gain Hands-On Experience**

   - Volunteer, freelance, or take on small projects to demonstrate your skills in a new context.

Communicating Your Skills Effectively

1. **Interviews**

   - Use the STAR method (Situation, Task, Action, Result) to describe how you've applied your skills successfully.

2. **Networking**

   - Share your career goals and highlight relevant skills during conversations with industry professionals.

3. **Portfolio or Case Studies**

   - Showcase your work through examples that demonstrate your transferable skills.

Maximizing the Value of Your Transferable Skills

1. **Highlight Versatility**

   - Use your diverse skills to show adaptability in a competitive job market.

2. **Demonstrate Value**

   - Connect your skills to the company's goals and challenges.

3. **Stay Open to Learning**

   - Pair your existing skills with a willingness to grow and evolve.

Section 1: Uncovering Hidden Treasures - Identifying and Categorizing Transferable Skills

Transferable skills are valuable assets that can be applied across industries and roles.

1. **Communication and interpersonal skills**

   - Verbal and written communication

   - Active listening

   - Conflict resolution

   - Team collaboration

2. **Problem-solving and analytical skills**

   - Critical thinking

   - Data analysis

   - Decision-making

   - Troubleshooting

3. **Leadership and management skills**

   - Strategic planning

   - Project management

- Team leadership
- Coaching and mentoring

4. **Creative and innovative skills**

- Idea generation
- Design thinking
- Product development
- Process improvement

5. **Technical and digital skills**

- Programming languages
- Software proficiency
- Data management
- Digital marketing

6. **Time management and organizational skills**

- Prioritization
- Scheduling
- Task management
- Goal setting

7. **Adaptability and flexibility**

- Change management
- Resilience
- Continuous learning
- Cultural competence

Section 2: Mapping Skills to New Career Paths - Exploring Industry and Functional Applications

Explore how your skills apply to different industries and roles.

1. **Industry-specific skills**

   - Healthcare

   - Finance

   - Technology

   - Education

2. **Functional skills**

   - Sales and marketing

   - Human resources

   - Operations management

   - Supply chain management

3. **Soft skills**

   - Emotional intelligence

   - Negotiation

   - Public speaking

   - Team building

4. **4. Hybrid skills**

   - Data-driven decision-making

   - Digital marketing analytics

   - Technical writing

   - Business development

Section 3: Highlighting Achievements and Experience – Showcasing Transferable Skills

Quantify and showcase your accomplishments.

1. **Creating a skills portfolio**

   - Documenting projects and achievements

   - Showcasing skills through case studies

   - Highlighting testimonials

2. **Developing a strong LinkedIn profile**

   - Optimizing your headline and summary

   - Showcasing skills and endorsements

   - Engaging with industry leaders

3. **Crafting a compelling resume**

   - Tailoring your resume to target roles

   - Highlighting transferable skills

   - Quantifying achievements

4. **Preparing impactful stories for interviews**

   - Using the STAR method

   - Showcasing skills in action

   - Highlighting achievements

Section 4: Bridging Skill Gaps - Strategies for Acquiring New Skills

Strategies for acquiring new skills.

1. **Online courses and certifications**

   - Platforms like Coursera, Udemy, and LinkedIn Learning

   - Industry-specific certifications

2. **Workshops and conferences**

   - Industry events

   - Networking opportunities

   - Skill-building sessions

3. **Mentorship and coaching**

   - Finding mentors

   - Coaching programs

   - Peer mentoring

4. **Volunteer and freelance work**

   - Applying skills in real-world settings

   - Building portfolio and network

   - Exploring new industries

Section 5: Real-Life Examples of Transferable Treasures - Inspiring Stories

Inspiring stories of skills leverage.

1. From teaching to corporate training

2. From military to project management

3. From sales to business development

4. From IT to data science

Section 6: Actionable Strategies for Leveraging Transferable Skills

Apply these tactics.

1. Skills assessment and inventory

2. Career path exploration

3. Networking and information gathering

4. Personal branding and online presence

5. Skill development planning

Section 7: Maximizing the Value of Your Transferable Treasures

Optimize your skills leverage.

1. Focus on high-demand skills

2. Develop a unique value proposition

3. Showcase transferable skills in interviews

4. Continuously update and refine skills

5. Leverage skills in entrepreneurial ventures

Section 8: Common Pitfalls to Avoid

Avoid these mistakes.

1. Underestimating transferable skills

2. Overemphasizing industry-specific skills

3. Ignoring soft skills

4. Failing to showcase achievements

5. Not continuously developing new skills

Key Takeaways

- Transferable skills are your greatest assets during a career transition.

- Identify your skills, translate them to align with your new career, and communicate them effectively.

- Invest in refining and building upon your skills to stay competitive.

- With a focus on your transferable treasures, you can confidently step into your new career.

Call to Action

Start uncovering your transferable treasures today. Reflect on your experiences, identify your strengths, and craft a compelling narrative to showcase your value. Take the first step toward your successful career transition with confidence!

Conclusion

Your existing skills, experience, and achievements are valuable treasures. By identifying, mapping, and leveraging these transferable treasures, you'll unlock new career opportunities and achieve success.

Actionable Exercises and Reflections

1. Conduct a skills inventory and categorize your transferable skills.

2. Explore new career paths

15

Career Reboot: Revitalizing Your Professional Journey

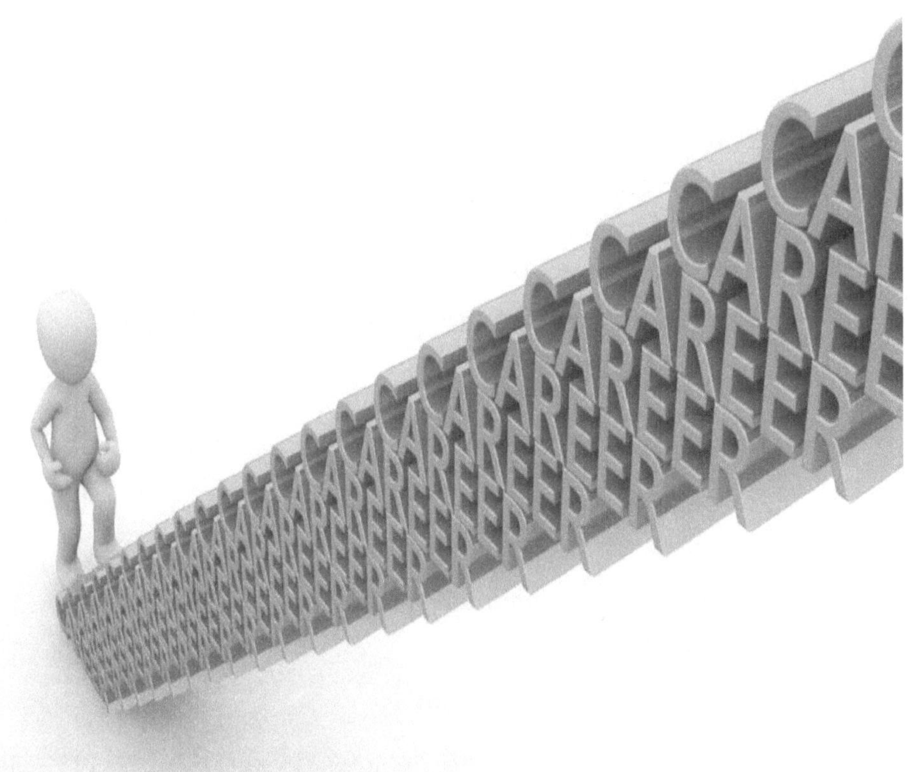

In Chapter 14, you discovered the power of transferable skills in propelling your career transition forward. Now, learn how to reboot your career, revitalizing your professional journey with purpose, passion, and renewed energy.

In today's fast-paced world, it's easy to feel stuck in your career, especially when you've been on the same path for years. A career reboot can breathe new life into your professional journey, enabling you to pursue new opportunities, regain enthusiasm, and align your work with your evolving goals. This chapter explores strategies for rejuvenating your career, reinvigorating your professional drive, and setting the stage for long-term fulfilment.

What is a Career Reboot?

A career reboot is essentially a fresh start, a conscious decision to re-examine your career path and make intentional changes to reinvigorate your professional life. This could involve shifting industries, advancing in your current field, or even pursuing a completely new direction. It's about realigning your work with your passions, strengths, and values.

Why You Might Need a Career Reboot

1. **Stagnation and Burnout**

   - If your job feels repetitive or you no longer find it fulfilling, it may be a sign to rethink your career.

   - Burnout can sap your energy, leaving you feeling disconnected and unproductive.

2. **Changing Personal Priorities**

   - As your personal life evolves, so do your professional needs and desires. A career reboot allows you to adjust your path to match your current goals.

3. **Shifting Industry Trends**

   - Economic changes, technological advancements, and industry disruptions can make your current role less relevant. A reboot can help you stay competitive.

4. **Unmet Potential**

   - You may have untapped skills or passions that could bring greater fulfilment or advancement if applied to a new or different career.

Steps to Reboot Your Career

1. **Reflect on Your Current Situation**

   - Take a step back and evaluate where you are in your career and where you want to go.

   - Ask yourself

     What do I enjoy about my current job?

     What's no longer serving me?

     What would I like to change?

2. **Assess Your Skills and Strengths**

   - Identify the skills you've developed and how they can be applied to new roles or industries.

   - Reflect on your achievements and how they align with your future aspirations.

3. **Identify What You Want from Your Next Career Move**

   - Define what you want in terms of work-life balance, compensation, professional growth, and job satisfaction.

   - Example: Are you looking for a more creative role, or do you want more responsibility and leadership opportunities?

4. **Consider Further Education or Training**

   - A career reboot may involve acquiring new skills or certifications to enhance your qualifications.

   - Example: If you're transitioning into a tech field, learning coding or data analytics could be beneficial.

5. **Explore Alternative Career Paths**

   - Research industries or roles you're curious about.

   - Network with professionals in these fields to get insight into their day-to-day work and required skills.

Overcoming Common Fears in a Career Reboot

1. **Fear of Starting Over**

   - It's natural to feel apprehensive about making a change, especially if you've invested years in your current career.

   - Remember that every step you've taken has provided valuable experience, and those skills are transferable.

2. **Fear of the Unknown**

   - Uncertainty can be intimidating, but embracing change is often the key to unlocking new opportunities.

   - Break your goals into small, manageable steps to make the transition less overwhelming.

3. **Fear of Financial Instability**

   - While a career reboot may involve a temporary financial adjustment, creating a financial cushion and a detailed plan can ease this fear.

   - Consider side gigs or freelance work as you transition to a new career path.

4. **Fear of Failure**

   - Understand that failure is often a stepping stone to success.

   - Many successful people faced setbacks before achieving their goals. Treat each failure as an opportunity for learning and growth.

Recharging Your Professional Identity

1. **Update Your Resume and LinkedIn Profile**

   - Tailor your resume to reflect your evolving skills, experiences, and new career goals.

   - Example: Highlight transferable skills and key achievements that align with your new direction.

2. **Craft Your Personal Brand**

   - Define how you want to be perceived in your field.

   - Develop a consistent narrative across your resume, LinkedIn, and personal website to communicate your professional identity clearly.

3. **Reignite Your Passion**

   - Rekindle the enthusiasm you once had for your work by exploring new challenges, joining industry groups, or volunteering in roles that align with your passions.

4. **Expand Your Network**

   - Reach out to professionals who can support your career reboot.

   - Attend networking events, engage in online communities, and seek out mentors who can provide guidance and encouragement.

Strategic Career Reboot Tips

1. **Leverage Your Transferable Skills**

   - As discussed earlier, identify the skills you've acquired throughout your career and explore how they can be applied to new roles.

   - Example: A project manager in a corporate setting might transition to leading projects in a nonprofit or government organization.

2. **Experiment Before Committing**

   - Test the waters before making a full commitment.

   - Consider freelancing, taking a part-time role, or volunteering in the field you want to move into. This can give you firsthand experience without making an immediate full-time shift.

3. **Stay Current**

   - Stay up-to-date on industry trends and technological advancements.

   - Example: Subscribe to industry newsletters, attend webinars, and complete relevant courses to keep your skills sharp.

4. **Be Patient and Persistent**

   - A career reboot doesn't happen overnight.

   - Be patient with the process, and keep making incremental progress toward your goals.

Real-Life Examples of Career Reboots

1. **The Corporate Lawyer Turned Social Entrepreneur**

   - A corporate lawyer tired of the long hours and high stress transitioned into nonprofit management, using her legal skills to advocate for underrepresented communities.

2. **The Accountant Turned Data Scientist**

   - An accountant with a passion for numbers and analysis pivoted to a data science career, taking online courses and completing a bootcamp to learn the necessary programming skills.

3. **The Teacher Turned Instructional Designer**

   - A teacher transitioned into instructional design, applying her deep knowledge of curriculum development to create e-learning courses for various industries.

Section 1: Recognizing the Need for a Career Reboot

Signs that indicate a career reboot is necessary:

1. Feeling stagnant or bored
2. Lack of challenge or growth opportunities
3. Mismatched values or culture
4. Unsatisfying work-life balance
5. Changing life circumstances or priorities
6. Limited autonomy or decision-making
7. Poor work environment or toxic culture
8. Insufficient recognition or rewards
9. Unfulfilling work or lack of purpose
10. Career plateau or limited advancement opportunities

Section 2: Reassessing Your Career Aspirations

Reflect on your:

1. Core values and priorities
2. Professional passions and interests
3. Long-term career goals
4. Personal definition of success
5. Ideal work environment and culture
6. Desired work-life balance
7. Preferred leadership style
8. Career legacy and impact
9. Skill utilization and development
10. Industry or sector preferences

Section 3: Revitalizing Your Professional Brand

Update and refresh your:

1. LinkedIn profile and online presence
2. Resume and portfolio
3. Networking strategy and connections
4. Personal website or blog
5. Social media profiles
6. Professional certifications and licenses
7. Online courses and training
8. Networking groups and associations
9. Personal brand statement
10. Career storytelling and elevator pitch

Section 4: Exploring New Career Pathways

Consider:

1. Industry shifts and emerging trends
2. Functional role changes
3. Entrepreneurial ventures
4. Freelance or consulting opportunities
5. Continuing education and certifications
6. Professional certifications and licenses
7. Online courses and training
8. Industry-specific conferences
9. Networking events and workshops
10. Informational interviews and shadowing

Section 5: Building a Support Network

Surround yourself with:

1. Mentorship and coaching
2. Peer support groups
3. Professional associations
4. Online communities and forums
5. Career counselling services
6. Industry experts and thought leaders
7. Networking groups and events
8. Supportive family and friends
9. Professional networking platforms
10. Personal development resources

Section 6: Creating a Career Reboot Plan

Develop a strategic plan with:

1. Short-term and long-term objectives
2. Actionable steps and timelines
3. Resource allocation and budgeting
4. Progress tracking and evaluation
5. Contingency planning
6. Skill development and training
7. Networking and relationship-building
8. Personal branding and marketing
9. Career exploration and research
10. Reflection and adjustment

Section 7: Overcoming Obstacles and Staying Motivated

Strategies to overcome:

1. Fear and self-doubt
2. Procrastination and inertia
3. External criticism and scepticism
4. Internal resistance and comfort zone
5. Maintaining momentum and motivation
6. Building resilience and adaptability
7. Celebrating small wins
8. Finding accountability and support
9. Practicing self-care and wellness
10. Staying focused on long-term goals

Section 8: Real-Life Examples of Successful Career Reboots

Inspiring stories of career transformation:

1. From corporate to non-profit
2. From entrepreneurship to intrapreneurship
3. From burnout to balanced career
4. From career break to successful re-entry
5. From industry switch to new opportunities

Section 9: Sustaining Career Growth and Renewal

Long-term strategies for continued growth:

1. Continuous learning and skill development
2. Networking and relationship-building
3. Adaptability and resilience
4. Purpose-driven work and social impact
5. Ongoing self-reflection and assessment
6. Career exploration and research
7. Professional certifications and licenses
8. Industry-specific conferences
9. Networking events and workshops
10. Personal development resources

Key Takeaways

- A career reboot is a powerful opportunity to reassess your goals and realign your professional life with your passions and strengths.

- Embrace change with an open mind, identify transferable skills, and seek out learning opportunities to enhance your qualifications.

- Overcome fears by planning strategically, experimenting with new roles, and building a support network.

- A career reboot requires patience, but it can lead to greater satisfaction, new challenges, and long-term success.

Call to Action

If you feel it's time to reset your career, take the first step today. Reflect on what you truly want from your work, identify the skills you bring, and explore new possibilities. The world is full of opportunities for those willing to embrace change—make your move and revitalize your professional journey!

Conclusion

Revitalizing your professional journey requires intentional effort and strategic planning. By recognizing the need for a career reboot, reassessing your aspirations, and building a support network, you'll propel yourself toward a fulfilling and purpose-driven career.

Actionable Exercises and Reflections

1. Identify signs that indicate a career reboot is necessary for you.

2. Reassess your core values, passions, and long-term goals.

3. Update your professional brand and online presence.

4. Explore new career pathways and opportunities.

5. Create a career reboot plan with actionable steps.

By applying these strategies, you'll successfully reboot your career, reigniting your passion, purpose, and professional growth.

Part 4

Achieving Career Growth and Fulfilment

16

Leadership Launchpad:
Building Skills for Career Advancement

In Chapter 15, you learned how to reboot your career, revitalizing your professional journey. Now, discover how to propel yourself to new heights by developing essential leadership skills.

Section 1: Understanding Leadership in the Modern Workplace

1. Defining leadership and its importance
2. Leadership styles and models (transformational, transactional, servant leadership)
3. Key characteristics of effective leaders (vision, communication, empathy)
4. The impact of technology on leadership (remote work, digital communication)
5. Globalization and cultural diversity in leadership
6. The role of ethics and social responsibility in leadership
7. Leadership development and succession planning

Section 2: Essential Leadership Skills for Career Advancement

1. Strategic thinking and planning (goal-setting, visioning)
2. Effective communication and collaboration (active listening, conflict resolution)
3. Emotional intelligence and empathy (self-awareness, emotional regulation)
4. Decision-making and problem-solving (critical thinking, creativity)
5. Coaching and mentoring (developing others, feedback)
6. Change management and adaptability (agility, resilience)
7. Building and leading high-performing teams (team dynamics, motivation)
8. Conflict resolution and negotiation (mediation, influence)
9. Time management and prioritization (productivity, focus)
10. Building a strong professional network

Section 3: Developing Leadership Skills through Practice and Experience

1. Leadership development programs and training (workshops, conferences)

2. Mentorship and coaching (finding mentors, peer mentoring)

3. Stretch assignments and projects (taking calculated risks)

4. Networking and building relationships (industry events, networking groups)

5. Volunteering for leadership roles (community service, committee leadership)

6. Seeking feedback and constructive criticism (360-degree feedback)

7. Reflecting on experiences and lessons learned (journaling, self-reflection)

Section 4: Leading in Times of Change and Uncertainty

1. Navigating ambiguity and uncertainty (flexibility, adaptability)

2. Building resilience and adaptability (self-care, stress management)

3. Communicating effectively in times of change (transparency, clarity)

4. Leading cross-functional teams (collaboration, influence)

5. Managing conflict and resistance (emotional intelligence, conflict resolution)

6. Fostering innovation and creativity (design thinking, experimentation)

7. Building a culture of trust and transparency (authenticity, vulnerability)

Section 5: Real-Life Examples of Successful Leadership

1. Inspirational stories of leadership transformation (career changes, industry shifts)

2. Case studies of effective leadership in action (successful projects, team achievements)

3. Interviews with successful leaders (leadership advice, best practices)

Section 6: Creating a Personal Leadership Development Plan

1. Assessing current skills and strengths (self-assessment, feedback)

2. Identifying areas for improvement and development (gap analysis)

3. Setting leadership development goals (SMART goals, objectives)

4. Developing a plan with actionable steps (implementation, timeline)

5. Tracking progress and evaluating success (metrics, feedback)

Section 7: Overcoming Leadership Challenges and Obstacles

1. Managing self-doubt and imposter syndrome (confidence-building, self-reflection)

2. Overcoming fear of failure (risk-taking, resilience)

3. Building confidence and assertiveness (communication skills, boundary-setting)

4. Navigating office politics (influence, networking)

5. Managing conflict and criticism (emotional intelligence, conflict resolution)

Section 8: Sustaining Leadership Growth and Development

1. Continuing education and training (workshops, conferences)

2. Networking and relationship-building (industry events, networking groups)

3. Seeking feedback and mentorship (peer mentoring, coaching)

4. Reflecting on experiences and lessons learned (journaling, self-reflection)

5. Staying adaptable and open to change (agility, resilience)

Conclusion

Leadership skills are essential for career advancement and professional growth. By understanding leadership, developing essential skills, and creating a personal development plan, you'll propel yourself to new heights.

Actionable Exercises and Reflections:

1. Assess your current leadership skills and strengths.

2. Identify areas for improvement and development.

3. Create a personal leadership development plan.

4. Seek feedback from mentors or peers.

5. Reflect on your leadership experiences and lessons learned.

By applying these strategies, you'll successfully launch your leadership journey, achieving career advancement and professional growth.

17

Balance and Harmony
Achieving Work-Life Integration

In Chapter 16, you discovered how to develop essential leadership skills for career advancement. Now, learn how to achieve balance and harmony in your life by integrating your personal and professional responsibilities.

Section 1: Understanding Work-Life Integration

1. Defining work-life integration and balance
2. The importance of balance for well-being and productivity
3. Challenges to achieving balance (technology, expectations)
4. Benefits of work-life integration (flexibility, resilience)
5. Historical perspective on work-life balance
6. Cultural and societal influences on balance
7. Individual differences in balance preferences

Section 2: Assessing Your Current Work-Life Balance

1. Evaluating priorities and values
2. Identifying areas for improvement
3. Assessing time management and boundaries
4. Recognizing signs of burnout and imbalance
5. Conducting a work-life balance audit
6. Seeking feedback from others
7. Reflecting on personal and professional goals

Section 3: Setting Boundaries and Priorities

1. Establishing clear work hours and expectations
2. Setting realistic goals and objectives
3. Learning to say "no" and delegate
4. Prioritizing self-care and wellness
5. Creating a boundary-setting plan
6. Communicating boundaries to others
7. Maintaining healthy relationships

Section 4: Effective Time Management Strategies

1. Scheduling and calendar management
2. Task prioritization and focus
3. Avoiding multitasking and distractions
4. Embracing flexibility and adaptability
5. Using technology to enhance productivity
6. Creating a daily routine
7. Managing meetings and communication

Section 5: Nurturing Relationships and Community

1. Building a support network
2. Communicating with family and friends
3. Joining community groups and organizations
4. Fostering meaningful connections
5. Nurturing romantic relationships
6. Building professional relationships
7. Maintaining social connections

Section 6: Practicing Self-Care and Wellness

1. Physical health and exercise
2. Mental health and mindfulness
3. Emotional intelligence and resilience
4. Spiritual growth and purpose
5. Self-care routines and rituals
6. Mindfulness practices
7. Seeking professional help

Section 7: Embracing Flexibility and Adaptability

1. Managing change and uncertainty
2. Being open to new opportunities
3. Developing resilience and coping skills
4. Maintaining a growth mindset
5. Embracing flexibility in work arrangements
6. Adapting to technological changes
7. Staying agile in a rapidly changing world

Section 8: Overcoming Obstacles to Balance

1. Managing technology and digital distractions
2. Overcoming perfectionism and guilt
3. Building confidence and assertiveness
4. Seeking support and resources
5. Managing conflict and stress
6. Creating a stress management plan
7. Practicing self-compassion

Section 9: Sustaining Work-Life Integration

1. Regular self-reflection and evaluation
2. Continuous learning and growth
3. Prioritizing relationships and community
4. Embracing flexibility and adaptability
5. Celebrating successes and milestones
6. Embracing challenges as opportunities
7. Maintaining a long-term perspective

Conclusion

Achieving work-life integration requires intentional effort and strategic planning. By understanding the importance of balance, assessing your current situation, setting boundaries, and prioritizing self-care, you'll create a harmonious and fulfilling life.

Actionable Exercises and Reflections:

1. Assess your current work-life balance.

2. Set realistic goals and priorities.

3. Establish clear boundaries and expectations.

4. Prioritize self-care and wellness.

5. Reflect on your progress and adjust.

By applying these strategies, you'll successfully integrate your personal and professional life, achieving balance, harmony, and well-being.

18

Success by Design:
Setting Goals and Tracking Progress

Section 1: Understanding the Power of Goal-Setting

1. The importance of goal-setting for success

2. Benefits of goal-setting (motivation, focus, clarity)

3. Types of goals (short-term, long-term, SMART)

4. Goal-setting frameworks (OKRs, Backward Goal-Setting)

5. Overcoming goal-setting obstacles (procrastination, fear)

6. Historical perspective on goal-setting

7. Scientific research on goal-setting effectiveness

8. Expert opinions on goal-setting best practices

Section 2: Setting Effective Goals

1. Identifying core values and priorities

2. Assessing strengths, weaknesses, opportunities, and threats (SWOT analysis)

3. Setting SMART (Specific, Measurable, Achievable, Relevant, Time-bound) goals

4. Creating a goal hierarchy (short-term, mid-term, long-term)

5. Writing a personal mission statement

6. Understanding the difference between goals and objectives

7. Creating a vision board for visual goal-setting

8. Incorporating mindfulness and intuition in goal-setting

Section 3: Breaking Down Big Goals into Smaller Ones

1. Creating an action plan

2. Setting milestones and deadlines

3. Identifying key performance indicators (KPIs)

4. Developing a task management system

5. Prioritizing tasks and focusing on high-impact activities

6. Using the Pomodoro Technique for productivity

7. Breaking down large projects into smaller tasks

8. Creating a schedule for goal achievement

Section 4: Tracking Progress and Staying Motivated

1. Creating a progress tracking system
2. Setting up accountability (accountability partner, journaling)
3. Celebrating milestones and successes
4. Overcoming obstacles and setbacks
5. Staying motivated (rewards, visualization, affirmations)
6. Using technology for progress tracking (apps, spreadsheets)
7. Creating a habit tracker for consistency
8. Incorporating mindfulness and self-compassion in progress tracking

Section 5: Adjusting and Refining Your Goals

1. Regularly reviewing progress
2. Assessing goal relevance and adjustability
3. Refining goals based on feedback and lessons learned
4. Embracing flexibility and adaptability
5. Maintaining a growth mindset
6. Using failure as a learning opportunity
7. Adjusting goals due to changing circumstances
8. Creating a contingency plan for unexpected setbacks

Section 6: Real-Life Examples of Successful Goal-Setting

1. Inspirational stories of goal achievement
2. Case studies of effective goal-setting
3. Expert interviews on goal-setting strategies
4. Historical examples of goal-setting success
5. Analyzing success stories for actionable insights

Section 7: Overcoming Common Goal-Setting Pitfalls

1. Avoiding unrealistic expectations
2. Overcoming procrastination and perfectionism
3. Managing fear and self-doubt
4. Building resilience and perseverance
5. Staying focused on long-term goals
6. Avoiding multitasking and distraction
7. Overcoming self-sabotaging behaviours
8. Creating a support system for goal achievement

Section 8: Sustaining Momentum and Achieving Long-Term Success

1. Maintaining momentum and motivation
2. Continuously learning and improving
3. Building a support network
4. Staying adaptable and open to change
5. Celebrating long-term successes
6. Reflecting on progress and adjusting strategy
7. Creating a legacy of success
8. Passing on knowledge and experience to others

Conclusion

Designing your success requires intentional goal-setting and progress tracking. By understanding the power of goal-setting, setting effective goals, breaking down big goals, tracking progress, and adjusting your approach, you'll achieve success and fulfilment.

Actionable Exercises and Reflections:

1. Set SMART goals for your personal and professional life.

2. Create an action plan with milestones and deadlines.

3. Develop a progress tracking system.

4. Identify potential obstacles and develop contingency plans.

5. Reflect on your progress and adjust your approach.

19

Navigating Transitions and Transformations: Embracing Change and Growth

Section 1: Understanding Transitions and Transformations

1. Defining transitions and transformations

2. Types of transitions (career, relationships, personal growth)

3. The importance of embracing change

4. Benefits of transformation (growth, renewal, innovation)

5. Overcoming resistance to change

6. Historical perspective on transformation

7. Scientific research on change management

8. Expert opinions on navigating transitions

Section 2: Recognizing the Need for Change

1. Identifying signs of stagnation
2. Assessing personal and professional dissatisfaction
3. Recognizing opportunities for growth
4. Understanding the impact of change on relationships
5. Building resilience and adaptability
6. Conducting a self-assessment
7. Seeking feedback from others
8. Reflecting on values and priorities

Section 3: Preparing for Transition

1. Setting clear intentions
2. Building a support network
3. Developing coping strategies
4. Managing fear and uncertainty
5. Creating a transition plan
6. Establishing a timeline
7. Identifying resources and tools
8. Developing a growth mindset

Section 4: Navigating the Transition Process

1. Embracing uncertainty and ambiguity
2. Managing emotions and stress
3. Maintaining focus and motivation
4. Building resilience and perseverance
5. Celebrating small wins

6. Practicing self-care

7. Seeking support

8. Reflecting on progress

Section 5: Transforming and Growing

1. Integrating new insights and skills

2. Developing a growth mindset

3. Building confidence and self-awareness

4. Embracing innovation and creativity

5. Sustaining momentum and progress

6. Overcoming self-doubt

7. Building resilience

8. Celebrating successes

Section 6: Overcoming Obstacles to Transformation

1. Managing self-doubt and fear

2. Overcoming external obstacles

3. Building resilience and perseverance

4. Maintaining focus and motivation

5. Celebrating successes

6. Learning from setbacks

7. Adapting to change

8. Seeking support

Section 7: Sustaining Growth and Transformation

1. Continuously learning and improving
2. Building a support network
3. Maintaining resilience and adaptability
4. Embracing lifelong learning
5. Passing on knowledge and experience
6. Reflecting on progress
7. Adjusting strategy
8. Celebrating milestones

Section 8: Real-Life Examples of Successful Transitions

1. Inspirational stories of transformation
2. Case studies of successful transitions
3. Expert interviews on navigating change
4. Historical examples of transformation
5. Analyzing success stories

Section 9: Best Practices for Navigating Transitions

1. Staying flexible
2. Building resilience
3. Embracing uncertainty
4. Seeking support
5. Celebrating successes
6. Learning from setbacks
7. Adapting to change
8. Maintaining focus

Conclusion

Navigating transitions and transformations requires courage, resilience, and determination. By understanding the process, preparing for change, and embracing growth, you'll transform your life and achieve personal and professional fulfilment.

Actionable Exercises and Reflections:

1. Identify areas for personal and professional growth.
2. Set clear intentions for transformation.
3. Build a support network.
4. Develop coping strategies.
5. Reflect on progress and adjust.

20

Sustaining Momentum and Achieving Long-Term Success

Section 1: Maintaining Momentum

1. The importance of sustaining momentum

2. Overcoming complacency and stagnation

3. Continuously setting new goals and challenges

4. Building resilience and adaptability

5. Celebrating milestones and successes

6. Reflecting on progress and adjusting strategy

7. Staying focused on long-term vision

8. Embracing lifelong learning

9. Creating a momentum mindset

10. Avoiding burnout and maintaining energy

Section 2: Strategies for Long-Term Success

1. Developing a growth mindset

2. Building a support network

3. Maintaining resilience and adaptability

4. Embracing innovation and creativity

5. Continuously learning and improving

6. Staying adaptable in a changing environment

7. Building strategic partnerships

8. Fostering a culture of excellence

9. Creating a success roadmap

10. Establishing accountability and tracking progress

Section 3: Overcoming Obstacles to Long-Term Success

1. Managing self-doubt and fear

2. Overcoming external obstacles

3. Building resilience and perseverance

4. Maintaining focus and motivation

5. Celebrating successes

6. Learning from setbacks

7. Adapting to change

8. Seeking support

9. Developing coping strategies

10. Practicing self-care

Section 4: Building a Legacy

1. Defining personal and professional legacy
2. Identifying core values and principles
3. Developing a legacy plan
4. Building a supportive community
5. Embracing mentorship and coaching
6. Creating a lasting impact
7. Reflecting on legacy and adjusting strategy
8. Celebrating legacy achievements
9. Establishing a legacy team
10. Documenting legacy stories

Section 5: Real-Life Examples of Long-Term Success

1. Inspirational stories of sustained success
2. Case studies of long-term achievement
3. Expert interviews on maintaining momentum
4. Historical examples of lasting impact
5. Analyzing success stories
6. Identifying key takeaways
7. Applying lessons learned
8. Creating a success journal
9. Reflecting on progress
10. Adjusting strategy

Section 6: Best Practices for Sustaining Momentum

1. Staying flexible and adaptable
2. Building resilience and perseverance
3. Embracing lifelong learning
4. Celebrating successes
5. Learning from setbacks
6. Adapting to change
7. Maintaining focus
8. Embracing innovation and creativity
9. Creating a growth culture
10. Fostering accountability

Section 7: Sustaining Momentum in Times of Change

1. Embracing uncertainty
2. Building resilience
3. Maintaining focus
4. Adapting to change
5. Seeking support
6. Learning from setbacks
7. Practicing self-care
8. Reflecting on progress
9. Adjusting strategy
10. Celebrating successes

Section 8: Creating a Sustainable Future

1. Building a sustainable business model
2. Embracing environmental sustainability
3. Creating social impact
4. Developing sustainable relationships
5. Fostering community engagement
6. Establishing sustainable practices
7. Measuring sustainability
8. Reporting sustainability progress
9. Celebrating sustainability successes
10. Continuously improving sustainability

Conclusion

Sustaining momentum and achieving long-term success require dedication, resilience, and a willingness to adapt. By maintaining momentum, embracing strategies for success, overcoming obstacles, building a legacy, and learning from real-life examples, you'll solidify your accomplishments and create a lasting impact.

Actionable Exercises and Reflections:

1. Reflect on your progress and adjust strategy.
2. Set new goals and challenges.
3. Build resilience and adaptability.
4. Celebrate milestones and successes.
5. Develop a legacy plan.

21

Pointers for Interns and Freshers Entering the Corporate World

Entering the corporate world as a fresher or an intern can be both exciting and challenging. Here are some actionable tips to help you navigate and thrive in your new environment:

1. **Master the Basics**

   - **Know Your Role:** Understand your job description, key responsibilities, and expectations. Seek clarity if you're unsure about anything.

   - **Learn Corporate Etiquette:** Be punctual, dress professionally, and maintain good manners in communication.

2. **Build a Positive Attitude**

   - **Be Open to Learning:** Treat every task as an opportunity to learn, even if it seems minor or unrelated to your career goals.

   - **Stay Adaptable:** Be willing to take on new challenges and adapt to changing situations.

3. **Prioritize Networking**

   - **Build Relationships:** Connect with colleagues across departments. Strong networks can help you in future career moves.

   - **Seek Mentors:** Identify experienced professionals who can guide you and provide valuable advice.

4. **Communicate Effectively**

   - **Ask Questions:** Don't hesitate to clarify doubts or seek feedback. It shows your willingness to learn.

   - **Practice Active Listening:** Pay attention during meetings and discussions to understand expectations and learn from others.

5. **Develop Professional Skills**

   - **Technical Skills:** Focus on improving the technical skills required for your role.

   - **Soft Skills:** Hone skills like communication, teamwork, and time management, which are critical for career growth.

6. **Embrace Feedback**

   - **Accept Criticism Gracefully:** Feedback is a tool for growth. Use it to identify areas for improvement.

   - **Seek Regular Feedback:** Don't wait for formal reviews—ask for informal feedback to stay on track.

7. **Set Goals and Track Progress**

   - **Short-Term Goals:** Identify what you want to achieve during your internship or probation period.

   - **Long-Term Vision:** Align your daily efforts with your broader career aspirations.

8. **Manage Time Efficiently**

   - **Prioritize Tasks:** Learn to distinguish between urgent and important tasks.

   - **Meet Deadlines:** Deliver your work on time to build a reputation for reliability.

9. **Be Proactive**

   - **Take Initiative:** Volunteer for projects or tasks that interest you and align with your strengths.

   - **Show Curiosity:** Research your company, industry trends, and competitors to add value to conversations.

10. **Maintain Work-Life Balance**

    - **Avoid Burnout:** Don't overextend yourself in an effort to impress. Maintain a healthy work-life balance.

    - **Practice Self-Care:** Regular exercise, proper sleep, and relaxation are essential for sustained performance.

11. **Leverage Technology**

    - **Use Productivity Tools:** Familiarize yourself with tools like project management software and collaboration platforms.

- **Stay Updated:** Keep learning about technologies and trends relevant to your industry.

12. **Observe and Learn**

- **Watch the Experts:** Learn from experienced colleagues by observing how they handle tasks and situations.

- **Understand Office Culture:** Adapt to the workplace culture while staying true to your core values.

13. **Showcase Integrity**

- **Be Honest:** Admit mistakes and take responsibility for them.

- **Stay Ethical:** Avoid office politics and maintain professional integrity at all times.

14. **Keep a Growth Mindset**

- **Be Resilient:** Accept that mistakes and failures are part of the learning process.

- **Seek Improvement:** Continuously work on enhancing your skills and knowledge.

15. **Evaluate Your Experience**

- **Reflect:** At the end of your internship or initial months, assess what you've learned and achieved.

- **Plan Next Steps:** Use the insights gained to shape the next phase of your career.

Final Thoughts

Entering the corporate world can be daunting, but with the right mindset and approach, you can make a lasting impression and build a strong foundation for your career. Remember, the initial phase is as much about learning as it is about contributing. Keep your focus, stay curious, and embrace every opportunity with enthusiasm!

22

Pointers for Mid-Level Professionals (Age 30-45)

At this stage in your career, you're likely juggling growing responsibilities, personal aspirations, and long-term career goals. Here are practical pointers to help you navigate this crucial phase:

1. **Refine Your Career Goals**

   - **Reassess Your Path:** Reflect on whether your current trajectory aligns with your personal and professional aspirations.

   - **Set Long-Term Goals:** Define where you want to be in the next 5-10 years and chart actionable steps to get there.

2. **Hone Leadership Skills**

   - **Develop Emotional Intelligence:** Cultivate empathy, self-awareness, and effective communication to lead teams better.

   - **Take Initiative:** Volunteer for leadership roles to gain experience managing projects and people.

3. **Expand Your Professional Network**

   - **Strengthen Connections:** Deepen relationships with colleagues, mentors, and industry peers.

   - **Attend Events:** Participate in conferences, seminars, and webinars to stay connected with industry trends.

4. **Prioritize Skill Development**

   - **Stay Relevant:** Invest in upskilling through courses, certifications, or workshops to keep pace with industry advancements.

   - **Master Soft Skills:** Enhance skills like negotiation, conflict resolution, and time management, which are critical for career progression.

5. **Manage Work-Life Integration**

   - **Set Boundaries:** Balance work demands with personal commitments to maintain mental and physical well-being.

   - **Embrace Flexibility:** Leverage remote work or flexible hours, if available, to support work-life harmony.

6. **Focus on Personal Branding**

    - **Showcase Expertise:** Publish articles, speak at events, or share insights on professional platforms like LinkedIn.

    - **Maintain Consistency:** Align your digital and offline presence with your professional image and goals.

7. **Evaluate Your Professional Value**

    - **Benchmark Salaries:** Research market standards to ensure your compensation reflects your skills and contributions.

    - **Ask for Feedback:** Regularly seek feedback from supervisors and peers to identify areas for improvement.

8. **Master Stakeholder Management**

    - **Understand Dynamics:** Learn to navigate office politics and build relationships with key stakeholders.

    - **Deliver Value:** Demonstrate your ability to drive results, which enhances your credibility and influence.

9. **Be Open to New Opportunities**

    - **Stay Agile:** Be prepared to adapt to new roles, industries, or projects that align with your growth aspirations.

    - **Consider Lateral Moves:** Shifting roles within your organization can diversify your experience and open new doors.

10. **Strengthen Financial Planning**

    - **Plan for the Future:** Invest in retirement funds, insurance, and savings to secure financial stability.

    - **Build an Emergency Fund:** Ensure you're financially prepared for unexpected career changes or personal challenges.

11. **Seek Mentorship and Mentorship Opportunities**

    - **Find a Mentor:** Continue learning from experienced professionals who can guide your decisions.

- **Mentor Others:** Sharing your knowledge with juniors can enhance your leadership skills and reputation.

12. **Embrace Change and Innovation**

- **Stay Curious:** Explore emerging technologies and industry trends to future-proof your career.

- **Drive Innovation:** Contribute ideas and solutions that improve processes or drive business growth.

13. **Improve Conflict Resolution Skills**

- **Stay Objective:** Approach conflicts professionally and focus on solutions, not blame.

- **Mediate Effectively:** Learn to handle workplace disagreements with diplomacy and tact.

14. **Focus on Health and Well-being**

- **Prioritize Fitness:** Incorporate regular exercise and a healthy diet into your routine.

- **Address Burnout:** Recognize signs of burnout early and take proactive steps to recharge.

15. **Prepare for Leadership Roles**

- **Think Strategically:** Transition from being task-focused to thinking about the bigger picture.

- **Influence Positively:** Learn to inspire and motivate teams to achieve organizational goals.

Final Thoughts

For mid-level professionals, this phase is about balancing stability with growth. Focus on refining your skills, expanding your network, and positioning yourself as a leader in your field. Remember, your experiences and decisions during this time will significantly impact the next phase of your career. Stay adaptable, proactive, and committed to continuous improvement!

23

Pointers for Lateral Entry Professionals (Age 45+)

Lateral entry professionals often bring a wealth of experience and expertise to their new roles, but transitioning into a different organization, industry, or role at this stage can pose unique challenges. Here are actionable pointers to help navigate this phase successfully:

1. **Leverage Your Experience**

   - **Highlight Achievements:** Showcase your career accomplishments and how they align with the organization's goals.

   - **Position Yourself as a Mentor:** Use your knowledge to guide younger colleagues, demonstrating your value as a team asset.

2. **Adapt to New Cultures and Technologies**

   - **Embrace Workplace Diversity:** Be open to learning from colleagues of different generations and backgrounds.

   - **Stay Tech-Savvy:** Update your skills in emerging tools, software, and technologies relevant to your new role or industry.

3. **Build Credibility Quickly**

   - **Listen and Learn:** Spend time understanding the organization's culture, goals, and challenges before proposing changes.

   - **Deliver Early Wins:** Focus on achieving measurable results early to establish your reputation in the new environment.

4. **Strengthen Emotional Intelligence**

   - **Understand Team Dynamics:** Build relationships with team members, showing respect for their ideas and contributions.

- **Manage Conflicts Effectively:** Use your experience to mediate disputes and maintain a harmonious workplace.

5. **Network Strategically**

   - **Reconnect with Industry Peers:** Reach out to former colleagues and contacts who can provide insights or collaboration opportunities.

   - **Engage Internally:** Build relationships with key stakeholders in your new organization to establish trust and alignment.

6. **Embrace Continuous Learning**

   - **Upskill Regularly:** Stay updated with certifications, workshops, or courses that enhance your relevance.

   - **Learn from Peers:** Be open to learning from younger colleagues who may have expertise in new areas.

7. **Balance Confidence with Humility**

   - **Acknowledge Your Strengths:** Draw confidence from your years of experience and proven track record.

   - **Stay Humble:** Approach the new role with curiosity and a willingness to adapt, avoiding the "know-it-all" trap.

8. **Focus on Effective Communication**

   - **Simplify Messages:** Use clear and concise communication to connect with diverse audiences.

   - **Solicit Feedback:** Regularly ask for feedback to refine your approach and demonstrate a growth mindset.

9. **Manage Expectations**

   - **Set Realistic Goals:** Understand that lateral transitions might involve a learning curve before you achieve significant milestones.

   - **Be Patient:** Building credibility and influence in a new role or industry takes time.

10. Showcase Adaptability

- **Be Open to Change:** Demonstrate your ability to adapt to new challenges, processes, and technologies.

- **Stay Flexible:** Show that you're willing to step out of your comfort zone when needed.

11. Align with Organizational Goals

- **Understand the Vision:** Familiarize yourself with the organization's mission and strategic priorities.

- **Add Value:** Position yourself as a solution-oriented professional who can contribute to achieving these goals.

12. Strengthen Work-Life Integration

- **Prioritize Health:** Maintain physical and mental well-being to sustain your energy and focus.

- **Balance Commitments:** Use this phase to align personal and professional goals for long-term satisfaction.

13. Address Stereotypes

- **Challenge Age Bias:** Prove your relevance through performance, not just experience.

- **Show Enthusiasm:** Counteract assumptions about being "set in your ways" by actively participating in new initiatives.

14. Seek Leadership Opportunities

- **Mentorship Roles:** Volunteer to mentor junior colleagues, leveraging your experience to build a collaborative environment.

- **Take Initiative:** Proactively contribute ideas and solutions to show your commitment to the organization's success.

15. Plan for the Future

- **Think About Legacy:** Focus on the long-term impact you want to leave in the role or organization.

- **Prepare for Transitions:** Whether considering retirement or future roles, have a clear plan for the next phase of your career.

Final Thoughts

Lateral entry professionals over 45 bring invaluable experience to their roles but must balance their expertise with a willingness to adapt and learn. By staying relevant, building relationships, and contributing strategically, you can ensure that this transition becomes a defining and fulfilling phase of your career journey.

24

Perfect Failures who rose to greatness

Narayana Murthy

Failure: Rejected for Funding in the Early Days of Infosys

- **Description:** Before founding Infosys, Murthy faced multiple rejections for funding from banks and investors. He started the company in 1981 with a loan of ₹10,000 from his wife.

- **Outcome:** Murthy grew Infosys into one of the largest IT services companies globally, symbolizing India's rise as a tech powerhouse.

P.V. Sindhu

Failure: Early Defeats in International Badminton

Description: Before becoming a world champion, P.V. Sindhu faced numerous losses in international tournaments. Her inability to secure major wins early in her career led to doubts about her consistency.

Outcome: Sindhu became the first Indian woman to win an Olympic silver medal in badminton and later clinched the gold medal at the BWF World Championships, making history for India.

Dhirubhai Ambani

Failure: Started as a Petrol Pump Attendant

Description: Before founding Reliance Industries, Dhirubhai Ambani worked as a petrol pump attendant in Yemen. He faced humble beginnings, financial struggles, and scepticism about his business ideas when he first started in India.

Outcome: Despite these challenges, Ambani built Reliance Industries, one of India's largest and most successful conglomerates, spanning sectors like energy, telecom, and retail. Failure: Started as a Petrol Pump Attendant

Description: Before founding Reliance Industries, Dhirubhai Ambani worked as a petrol pump attendant in Yemen. He faced humble beginnings, financial struggles, and scepticism about his business ideas when he first started in India.

Outcome: Despite these challenges, Ambani built Reliance Industries, one of India's largest and most successful conglomerates, spanning sectors like energy, telecom, and retail.

Vera Wang

Failure: Failed Olympic Figure Skater

- **Description:** Wang was a competitive figure skater who failed to make the U.S. Olympic team. After retiring from skating, she worked as a fashion editor at Vogue but was passed over for the editor-in-chief position.

- **Outcome:** At age 40, Wang pivoted to designing wedding gowns, building a multimillion-dollar brand and becoming one of the most prominent designers in the world.

Michael Jordan

Failure: Cut from High School Basketball Team

- **Description:** As a sophomore, Jordan was cut from his high school basketball team, which deeply discouraged him. However, this failure motivated him to train harder.

- **Outcome:** Jordan became one of the greatest basketball players of all time, with six NBA championships and numerous accolades to his name.

Dr. A.P.J. Abdul Kalam

Failure: SLV-3 Rocket Failure

- **Description:** Early in his career as a scientist, Dr. Kalam was involved in the launch of India's first Satellite Launch Vehicle (SLV-3), which failed to deploy the satellite. The failure was a significant setback for ISRO and his team.

- **Outcome:** Dr. Kalam used this failure as a stepping stone to later lead successful missions, including the development of India's ballistic missile and satellite programs. He went on to become the "Missile Man of India" and a beloved President.

Shah Rukh Khan

Failure: Struggles as a Young Actor

- Description: Before becoming the "King of Bollywood," Shah Rukh Khan faced numerous rejections and doubts about his potential in the film industry. His early life was marked by personal losses, including the death of his parents.

- Outcome: Despite these challenges, Khan became one of the most successful and influential actors in the world, earning accolades and a massive global fanbase.

Mahendra Singh Dhoni

Failure: Rejected by Railways Cricket Team

- Description: Before becoming one of the most celebrated cricketers in India, Dhoni faced rejection from the Railways cricket team and worked as a ticket collector. His unconventional techniques were often questioned.

- Outcome: Dhoni became one of India's most successful cricket captains, leading the team to multiple international victories, including the 2007 T20 World Cup and the 2011 ICC Cricket World Cup.

Kiran Mazumdar-Shaw

Failure: Struggles to Start Biocon

- Description: As a young entrepreneur, Mazumdar-Shaw faced scepticism for being a woman in the biotech industry and struggled to secure funding and support for her company, Biocon. Many doubted the feasibility of her business model.

- Outcome: Biocon grew into one of India's largest biopharmaceutical companies, earning her the title of "India's Biotech Queen" and making her one of the country's wealthiest self-made women.

Conclusion

These stories of failure and redemption from India illustrate that setbacks are not the end of the road. Each of these individuals used their failures as opportunities for learning and growth, ultimately achieving greatness in their respective fields. Their journeys remind us that perseverance, resilience, and self-belief can overcome even the most daunting obstacles.

About the Author

Anupam Peter is a renowned career guidance expert, empowers individuals to achieve their professional aspirations. With over 10+ years of experience, Anupam Peter has established himself as a trusted authority in career development, coaching, and leadership.

Professional Background

A seasoned career coach, he has guided numerous individuals across industries, from fresh graduates to senior executives. His expertise spans career transition, talent management, and professional networking.

Personal Philosophy

"[Anupam Peter] believes meaningful careers are built on self-awareness, resilience, and strategic decision-making. He is passionate about empowering individuals to unlock their potential and achieve fulfilment in their professional journeys."

www.ingramcontent.com/pod-product-compliance
Lightning Source LLC
Chambersburg PA
CBHW031126130726
47988CB00006B/2246